CARMEL, LAND OF THE SOUL

Carmel,
Land of the Soul

Living Contemplatively in Today's World

CAROLYN HUMPHREYS

ST PAULS

Library of Congress Cataloging-in-Publication Data

Humphreys, Carolyn.
 Carmel, land of the soul: living contemplatively in today's world /
Carolyn Humphreys.
     p. cm.
Includes bibliographical references (p.   ).
 ISBN 0-8189-0946-3
1. Christian life—Catholic authors. 2. Carmelites—Spiritual life.
I. Title.

BX2350.3.H86 2003
248.4'82—dc21
                                    2002156620

Produced and designed in the United States of America by the
Fathers and Brothers of the Society of St. Paul,
2187 Victory Boulevard, Staten Island, New York 10314-6683,
as part of their communications apostolate.

ISBN: 0-8189-0946-3
ISBN: 978-0-8189-0946-7

Printing Information:

Current Printing - first digit	2	3	4	5	6	7	8	9	10

Year of Current Printing - first year shown

2008	2009	2010	2011	2012	2013

Table of Contents

Foreword ix

1. As Carmelite Pilgrims 1

2. Labors Along the Way...21

3. Food for the Journey...39

4. Desert Lands 51

5. Traveling Light...73

6. Body and Soul 93

7. Stewards of Conservation..................................115

8. On the Mountain 143

9. The Alpine Peaks...169

Bibliography 195

My heartfelt gratitude is extended to the following persons
for their help in making this book a reality:

Penny Brown, OCDS,

Doreen Glynn Pawski, OCDS, MA,

Milton Gray, OCDS,

Al Sieracki, O.Carm.,

Barbara Donley, OCDS, CRNA,

David Centner, OCD,

Joan Carsola, T.O.Carm.,

John Gannon, OCDS and his wife

Marette Gannon, OCDS, RN

Foreword

In our day, as perhaps never before, we have access to a vast amount of information. We have data banks bursting with information about every conceivable item. Our minds and emotions are barraged with an array of knowledge on every possible theme.

How are we to cope with all this? How are we to find time for reflection on the deeper things in life? In particular, how do we find the calm, the peace and tranquillity vital for living with a deep sense of God's presence and of his love for us?

This is a monumental challenge: on the one hand to appreciate and accept lovingly the gifts of God through the advance of technology, and yet not to be imprisoned and bewildered by it all.

Allied to this expansion of knowledge is a painful and tragic ignorance of what goes on within ourselves: the consciousness that is vital to the perception of God in our lives. *Noverim Te, noverim me* (May I know You, may I know myself). St. Augustine's cry of the heart so long ago is an insightful summing up of the goal of our spiritual journey.

Noverim me — may I know myself — is of particular interest to Carmelites. Their approach to God through self-knowledge and contemplative prayer has typified the Order throughout the centuries. It has gathered momentum with the passing of years, until contemplative prayer is almost synonymous with the Carmelite charism.

Carmel, Land of the Soul is written by a Secular Carmelite, author of *From Ash to Fire*, a volume which appeared a few years ago. In various chapters, beginning with As Carmelite Pilgrims, followed by: Food for the Journey, Traveling Light, Desert Lands, etc., and culminating in Alpine Peaks — the author offers guidelines and admonitions for our spiritual journey. It is manifestly the fruit of deep experience in prayer, full of wise observations and counsels. The book will surely be of signal help to all those who have set their feet resolutely on the way to God. It will help them persevere in their pilgrimage, until, as the Carmelite liturgy puts it: "They come to the Holy Mountain, Christ the Lord" the goal of all our contemplative strivings.

Father Michael Buckley, OCD
Recently Provincial Delegate
Secular Discalced Carmelites
OCD Western Province, USA

CARMEL, LAND OF THE SOUL

1

As Carmelite Pilgrims

> When you wonder about the mystery of yourself, look to
> Christ who gives you the meaning of life. When you won-
> der what it means to be a mature person, look to Christ who
> is the fullness of humanity. Because actions speak louder
> than words, you are called to proclaim by the conduct of
> your daily lives that you really do believe that Jesus is the
> Lord.   *John Paul II*

Our era in the history of humanity is unlike any other. Never
before have we had access to so much information about discoveries and events in the world around us. Special reports bring
instantaneous coverage of news, near and far, to our homes. Data
banks burst with information about every conceivable item. High
technology opens doors to expansive regions where no one has
gone before.

Nevertheless, the reality that underlines our vast accumula-
tion of information concerning the world is a painful ignorance
of what is going on inside ourselves. When humankind pursues
them in a life-enhancing context, mechanistic expansions in the
outer world uphold humanistic values and concerns. However,
for optimal development the journey outward must link with the
journey inward. In a pastoral letter marking the international year
of youth in 1985, the Irish Catholic bishops said: "The only God
worth believing in is the God who believed enough in people to

die for us. The only God worth living for is the one who called us to live with him, through dark faith in this life and beyond death to face to face fullness. The only God worth searching for is the one who searched for us and still struggles within us, in order that we may become more free to love."

Currently, there appears to be a renewed interest in prayer and the spiritual realm in many parts of the world. People seem to be turning away from an agitated and wasteful lifestyle, with its consequent consumer mentality, to something deeper that is of lasting value. They want to locate the treasures in a back to basics life and attain some semblance of tranquillity. Above all, they seem to cry out for a personal relationship with God.

So begins the most captivating and mystifying adventure known to men and women. The spiritual journey is the oldest and longest that can be made in this world and, unlike any other, it continues in the world to come.

Genuine commencement on the Christian way begins with the reception of the waters of baptism. The journey itself is not possible without absolute faith in God; and we learn about faith and God through reading Sacred Scripture, growing through the sacraments, and living as followers of Jesus.

The language of the interior life, which is another name for the spiritual journey, is prayer. In the depths of prayer we commune most profoundly with God, and prayer links us to God and others in extraordinary ways. Communication in prayer has many modes, the most basic of which are adoration, praise, contrition, supplication and thanksgiving. These elements of prayer are at the heart of the interior life. Because the forces of prayer move us from the outskirts of our ego selves to the inroads of our true selves in Christ, it takes unwavering perseverance to stick with the work of honest, day-to-day prayer. However, with day-by-day graces from the Holy Spirit, prayer transforms us into a new life in Christ.

The Church is a fellowship of all who are bound together by their love for Jesus Christ. Through viable sacramental and virtuous lives, we are united by our profession of faith and nourished in our Christian faith. As people of God, we are the Church. We participate in our call to holiness through our uniqueness and our Christian response to the various circumstances in our lives.

To be a Catholic Christian is a sublime call. We represent Jesus in the world because we are the Church in the world. Through our knowledge, skills and social contacts, we infuse the mission of the Church into secular society. As people of God we bear witness to our faith through love. We give love away and thus spread it around to places where it is unknown. The master of prayer and mystical poet, John of the Cross said: "Where there is no love, put love and you will draw love out." Love connects us with each other, all creation and God.

Although love is the most important quality of human existence, we can never adequately define or understand it. We show love in many ways, but its full comprehension is an elusive mystery, known only by God. Dwight Moody gives us these expressions of love: "Joy is love exalted. Peace is love in repose. Long suffering is love enduring. Gentleness is love in society. Goodness is love in action. Faith is love on the battlefield. Meekness is love in school and temperance is love in training." These are beautiful definitions of love, yet its essence is yet to be fathomed. Indeed, love is fathomless, but is the most overwhelming growth experience in which we partake. A person who has nothing or who lives in the most wretched of situations can be rich in the wisdom of love. Love finds its deepest meaning in our spiritual being as it is stronger than death. Indeed, the mental image of a loved one can be more real than his or her physical presence, the immediate presence of others or adverse surroundings.

As people of God, we journey with Jesus to the Father with guidance from the Holy Spirit. We all move toward the same goal. However, as love takes on various forms for each individual, so does the spiritual journey.

Within the Church, there is a beautiful diversity of schools of spirituality. The different religious orders offer the people of God a variety of directions and charisms. The plan of life and disciplines by which the members live are described in their rule and constitutions. The members strive for Christian perfection, which means perfection in love in accordance with their rule. Each order offers different kinds of membership. Friars or monks are priests or brothers. Nuns are cloistered contemplatives while the sisters are engaged in active apostolates. Seculars or lay members are married, single, or diocesan clergy, who live the charisms of the Order in the midst of the world. Two time-honored saints who lived the Dominican charism in the world are Catherine of Siena and Rose of Lima. Although there are various kinds of membership, each member shares in full the Order's spiritual heritage, its ideals, its grace and its mission in the Church.

The Carmelites do not have a "classic" rule as do the Benedictines or Franciscans; nor do they have a founder such as Dominic or Augustine. The Carmelite Order is named after a mountain; Mount Carmel in Haifa, Israel. This mountain offers a great challenge to those who wish to climb it.

A Brief History

To live a life of quiet prayer was the major impetus that brought the Carmelite Order into existence. A small group of pilgrims, merchants, crusaders and soldiers began to settle on Mount Carmel in Palestine around the year 1135. These men from western Europe wanted a simple and solitary life so they could sincerely seek God. They lived in huts and caves and combined solitary prayer with manual work on their land. The Eucharistic Sacrifice brought them together in their chapel which was dedicated to Mary, the mother of Jesus. This chapel became a place of pilgrimage and the men became known as the brothers of Our Lady of Mount Carmel.

In 1209, the brothers asked their bishop, Albert, patriarch of Jerusalem, to write a rule based on their way of life. A brief document of some twenty-four paragraphs became known as the primitive rule of Carmel or the rule of St. Albert.

Due to increased hostilities in the Holy Land, the brothers began their migration to various areas in Europe around 1239. Their life of solitude on the mountain changed to community life in the city. In 1247 their rule was adapted to accommodate these changes. At this time the Carmelites became a mendicant Order similar to the Franciscans and Dominicans. They were now itinerant friars in the marketplace.

In 1452 the privilege of aggregating convents of nuns and tertiaries (now known as secular members) was granted to the Carmelite Order by Pope Nicholas V. By the sixteenth century, the convents of nuns and monasteries of friars were numerous. They lived according to a mitigated rule. Teresa de Cepeda y Ahumada entered such a convent in Avila, Spain in October of 1536. The name of the convent was the Carmel of the Incarnation.

Teresa was born in Spain on the eve of the Reformation in 1515. She lived through troubled times, much like our own. Her love for Jesus guided her to establish a renewed form of life in the Carmelite Order. She modified the rule of St. Albert for women and gave the Church a lifestyle that embodied deep love and intense prayer. Teresa believed there was no better way to God than the way of prayer.

Teresa established several convents of nuns. Along with her associate, John of the Cross, she restored the primitive rule to her newly founded houses of friars. Before she died she had the consolation of seeing her Discalced Carmelite friars and nuns established as a separate province of the Carmelite Order. Discalced means unshod or with sandaled feet, which was a sign of poverty in those days.

Today there are two Orders within the Carmelite family: the ancient observance, and the discalced (also known as the

Teresian reform). Each order has its own friars, nuns and secular members.

The traditions and spirit of Carmel come from Elijah the prophet, and Mary, the mother of God. Elijah represents zeal, leadership, penance and prophetic witness to the living God. His life is an excellent example of what it means to be a prophet. He was faithful to religious traditions and creative in applying them to the problems of his time. The prophetic dimension of Elijah is a challenge for all Carmelites, because it encourages the members to be aware and informed of the problems of their time. He inspires Carmelites to confront them in accord with the doctrines of their faith. As did Elijah, today's Carmelite seeks the face of God in solitude and brings him to the marketplace with ardor.

Mary balances Elijah's fiery zeal and passion with quiet contemplation and deep pondering. She embodies the fullness of the contemplative life and is the finest example of unwavering faith, steadfast love and wholehearted trust in God. Mary teaches us to be still and silent about the unknown and unresolved areas in our lives. She asks us to ponder deeply and nudges us toward her son. For Carmelites, this means standing with Mary at the foot of the cross.

As Love in the World

Carmelites live their spirituality within society for the good of society. They believe in the goodness of the world and the good things in the world, because they know from whom that goodness comes. The spiritual life is the root and ground of all life. The more strongly Carmelites are drawn to God, the more they must go out of themselves. This cardinal precept is necessary in order to channel divine life into the world.

Fidelity to the Carmelite way of life enables a person to be more Christlike and loving within his or her surroundings.

If there is an opposite effect, the interpretation of the Carmelite way is flawed. The duties of Carmel should not interfere with or cause conflict in a person's interpersonal relationships. The rights and feelings of others are of utmost concern. A true vocation to Carmel enhances relationships and combines the healthy values of the world with the charisms of Carmel. Faithful living of the Carmelite way should unobtrusively blend with daily activities. The way of Carmel directs members to offer and execute routine tasks for the love of God, the concerns of the Church and for the world.

Union with God through love and prayer is the primary charism of Carmel. People can find God's presence in many places; however, the first priority of the Carmelite is to find his presence within. To find God in the quiet and mysterious regions within oneself resembles exploring a dark cave. A God-seeking Carmelite cannot see in the interior of the huge, dark, dank cave, but he or she enters it with confidence, trust and hope. The cave represents a realm of God inside of a person. It is massive, with hidden passages, secret caverns and unexpected findings. About midpoint inside the seeker bypasses the desire to attain specific information about God or capture him by certain spiritual techniques. A pioneer in Carmel truly seeks the living God. The more a person ventures into the depths of the cave, the easier it will be to let God do what he wants in his intangible, incomprehensible way.

As the journey continues, Carmelites grow in their companionship with Jesus. They yearn to express the praying Christ to the world. A simple attention and quiet awareness of God's presence within sanctifies the work they do. Carmel has no specific external apostolates for its members in the world. The basic thrust of Carmel is an ongoing development of the interior life which is made manifest by growth in common sense love and service to others. Through this, members give honor and glory to God. Consistently and quietly they give witness, like burning incense, to the beauty of the interior life to the world. Carmelites in the world are not privileged Christians or better than their neighbors. Rather, they are Catholic Christians who freely choose to matriculate in the Carmelite school of spirituality. To live as a pilgrim of prayer in the midst of the world is a vigorous, continual challenge to the whole person.

Of all human experiences, prayer is the simplest and the most profound. The school of Carmel provides people with a means to explore their internal depths for a lifetime of prayer. Two primary necessities in Carmel are silence and solitude. Places and times for silence and solitude are not easy to find in modern society. God-seekers on Mount Carmel face the battle and babble of the ages as they continually turn from peripheral living to searching for God. To live in the midst of the world and be not of it is an ongoing challenge. Silence and solitude are supports that link the whole Carmelite family together. No one is really alone as he or she strives to pray, think with the teachings of Jesus, and respond as one imagines Jesus might have done.

Interior silence and solitude are needed as guides to God that go beyond the absence of noise or people. Self-knowledge and faith are built on these supportive structures which are as lattices for growth in giving and receiving. Carmelites do not forget others; instead they stand alone in God's presence for others. Prayers for people are offered and a greater sense of God's goodness is received. God is sought through quiet waiting and pondering, and is received by unknowingly drawing closer to Jesus. Eventually, Carmelites find themselves without masks, adornments or devotional accretions and experience true freedom in the peace of Christ. Teresa said it well: "We need no wings to go in search of him, but have only to find a place where we can be alone and look upon his presence within us."

Silence and solitude are rarely comfortable. Yet, in times of darkness and ambiguity, they embrace patience and trust with no words. The mysteries of life become more profound, and frustrations mellow with the seemingly slow work of God, as an individual moves deeper into silence and solitude. Sometimes seekers are unable to find answers after a long search and only discover more questions at the end. It is soon learned that Carmelites are seekers of God who are never satisfied. Those in Carmel are sometimes spiritually uprooted, tossed about, and feel like strangers in a strange land. God does not seem to respond to their plaintive entreaties. Still, the silence and solitude that accompany a Carmelite pilgrim's search resemble an unknown wilderness with wild wonderful discoveries, and mysterious adventures.

Joined together, silence and solitude provide a climate of authentic presence. They prime hearts to listen and probe the deep truths of God. Together they show how everything in the spiritual and physical world interconnect. Indeed, the dedication and perseverance of solitary contemplatives scattered across the land, will have a cumulative effect on the world. Silence and solitude are the wings of prayer that provide the energy for service. They help a pilgrim of prayer reach into the depths of his or her heart and soul and profoundly experience the joy and suffering in life. The Carmelite, Thérèse of Lisieux, who was spoken of by Pope Pius X as "the greatest saint of modern times" counsels a modern pilgrim: "Do not be afraid to tell Jesus that you love him, even if you do not feel that you love him. Prayer is a cry of gratitude and love in the midst of trial as well as in joy." Silence and solitude open an individual up by broadening and deepening his or her strengths and vulnerabilities. Together they fortify a Carmelite with mature faith and present the challenges of the unknown in a clearer perspective. It is soon learned that magical idleness, withdrawal from life, introspection, visions or revelations are not waves in the sea of contemplative prayer. Silence and solitude clear the deck for us to view unclaimed and uncharted lands barren of superstitions, fantasy or mythical elements that may have invaded our faith or religious practices. Furthermore, they liberate seekers from themselves, so they may place another's burdens at the center of their being. Gently, Carmelites hold others in their hearts as they tenderly pray for them. Through their tenderheartedness, they become as quiet and receptive as possible to practical applications that God may provide.

In our age of religious activism and expanding parish ministries, the need for personal spiritual growth is greater now than ever before. Silence and solitude are unclaimed treasures within this realm. They bear witness to the primacy of the spiritual and the mystical charisms of the Church. Through fidelity to prayer, within an atmosphere of silence and solitude, Carmelites strive to become the people God has called them to be. When they are alone with God they become more attentive to his gentle whispers. God's presence within each one of us is unique as each individual is unique. With gifts from grace and the ongoing realization of our spiritual potential we find our true reality in God's novel expressions within us.

Know Thyself

Carmelite spirituality generates a greater openness to the beauty and brokenness of life. Indeed, those in Carmel become more vulnerable to wounds on their way to God. Wounds break Carmelite pilgrims, then aid them in blessed, new growth. Knowledge of the good and evil in their past and present may be unpleasant on the surface, but reveal a certain wisdom at a deeper level. Introspection helps the pilgrims of Carmel realize how intimately God loves them. Furthermore, it helps them love others. It goes beyond the fear of being hurt again, and the fear of the unknown that lies ahead. As seekers in Carmel learn more about themselves, they become more open and yielding to God's mysterious actions. They allow themselves to be loved by God because of who he is and who they are, not because of what they get from God or what they do. God's beautiful and continual invitation to all people is to let them be loved by him. Prayer, grace and Christian principles, permeated by God's love, are guides by which they make sound and life-sustaining decisions. The measure of peoples' closeness to God is the measure of faith from which they let themselves be loved by him. Faith gives Carmelites the stamina to stand by their convictions, especially when they receive strong opposition from others.

The beauty of Carmel may be analogous to sitting on the porch in the evening and appreciating being there. This involves no effort or work, just a simple, wakeful presence. There are no hidden agendas for mystical sanctity or elaborate plans for spiritual success. Carmelite pilgrims are simply themselves. In Carmel, the essence of the present moment is sacred. Pilgrims become gently appreciative of God's presence in themselves and in everything that surrounds them.

Carmel offers the "something more" in life which strives for a combination of the highest attainable union with the infinite God and the deepest venture on the face of the earth. The spirit of Carmel urges pilgrims forward on this concurrent quest: An inner journey which must be companioned by an outer journey. One cannot survive without the other. Self-knowledge, which is collected along the inner journey through self and soul to God, takes pilgrims out of themselves in order to give themselves in selfless love to others. Energy for this bilateral movement is activated by tapping the wisdom of the soul and the fountain of grace. This remarkable energy transports pilgrims to a deeper level of existence than society recognizes. For truly, God is beyond the boundaries of societal or scientific explanations and seeking him becomes a ceaseless, sacred passion.

Carmelites find God everywhere, in the profoundest of mysteries, the simplest of elements, within the regions of the heart or in the outer limits of space. Like flowers that grow near the highway, pilgrims in Carmel rest, assured of God's providence. They brave inclement weather knowing Carmel's vision will see them through the blizzards of life. They remain steadfast in God's eternal love as the ground around them is littered by worldly travelers. They realize that the beauty of self-esteem is not possible without a viable spiritual dimension. Each flower is lovely in its own right. Carmel's personal expression of life views individuals as respectable, irreplaceable and unique; this takes permanent pride of place over society's expression of existence that views people as fatuous, expendable objects. Carmel reaches into the soul and grasps how faith grows through enlightenment and achievements as well as deficiencies and failings. Indeed, whatever happens to the Carmelite has validity and value.

Like a sharp razor blade, Carmel cuts into the deepest depths of the soul. With perseverance in prayer the treasures of the soul unfold and are trusted. New discoveries about a person's precious uniqueness are revealed. As growth in reverence for self increases, so does reverence for all humanity. At the deep levels of fellowship in Carmel, souls touch souls as love passes between and through them. Love pulses from the utmost depths of each soul wherein lies a pristine reservoir of God's omnipotent love.

In order to keep the body, mind and soul working, the Carmelite knows that each must be nourished and exercised. Powerful interactive communication exists between the body, mind and soul, and their effects, one upon the other and as a total unit, are a ripe area for deeper exploration. The body is home for the soul during its earthly stay, and it responds to an overwhelming amount of sensory stimuli in varying ways. The mind has an incredible influence on the body, can reach beyond what it understands as it guides and feeds the soul. The soul sends subtle messages to the mind and body and is the source for inner beauty. Whatever affects the body affects the mind and soul as well, even though human senses and perceptions are limited and cannot tell where the mind or soul begins or ends.

Careful preparation is one requirement for a Carmelite's pursuit of God. Travelers in the land of Carmel receive sustenance from the staples of life. These staples meet survival needs basic to Christians, but more so to Carmelites as they perpetually seek

God on a rough mountain terrain.

Carmel is a soul-stirring adventure as its charisms permeate the nitty gritty details of life. A substantial part of this book identifies and develops primordial staples which are essential to love and life. They are as essential to love and life as breath. These primordial staples are channels that transport us to the heavens as long as they increase our sensitivity on earth. Attention is given to life's primordial staples because they filter through and affect all dimensions of existence. They are important in ways known and unknown as they converge in a faith that binds Carmelites to God and all people. With support from the staples of life, Carmelite pilgrims climb the mountain of faith that connects earth with heaven and humanity with God. Mount Carmel invites the reader to experience the expedition of a lifetime and beyond.

A pioneer with an authentic attraction to Carmel has what no one can give, save God. God calls hearty pioneers to hike on Mount Carmel by fidelity to interior prayer and instills in them the desire to trod this lifelong trail. Fidelity to the call of lifelong interior prayer is a time-honored and lofty commitment. After the novelty wears off, there are no more prolonged daydreams about experiencing some courtly mystical rendezvous, becoming a renowned contemplative sage or blazing a new trail on the spiritual frontier. Carmelites do not fancy that their prayers will save the world, or that they are privileged or prestigious spiritual persons. These fantasies soon melt in the heat of reality. If the neophyte Carmelite's feet are on firm spiritual ground, any alluring fantasy does not last for long. It is an illusion of great error to think, even for a moment, that Carmelites are better or more holy than others. Aged and timeworn Carmelite pioneers can reassure the neophyte that Carmelites are not even necessarily better at prayer than others.

Carmelites are a heterogeneous group who come from different social, cultural, educational and political situations. Carmel's unity lies in the richness of the interior life, which members find at the deep center of their being. The Carmelite structure on which they base their lives may be likened to a rose trellis. Its purpose is to support, yet it allows freedom for growth. Carmelite teachings are as signposts on the trellis. They guide the lives of pilgrims toward an ever-increasing consciousness of the presence of God. Anything in their lives can be transformed. A particular lifestyle may change, but this is not a primary concern. However, the Christian quality within the lifestyle is. The signposts to which Carmel points always direct people to transformation through the love of God. This takes place within the context of their way of life. Its baseline is the value and virtue of the person as he or she lives within the framework of the love of God.

Carmel has been likened to a garden, a sanctuary of peace, hidden in the depths of an individual. No matter where a person is in time or in place, he or she may take refuge in the garden, to dwell in its serenity and embrace the world with prayer. Prayer is so very good for the growth of one's soul and for all the souls in the world. In the tranquil garden of Carmel, wisdom is cultivated into the land of the soul. Through wisdom, a thriving soul keeps body and mind together. Gifts from the soul keep elements in a person's values, goals and activities neither excessive nor ungrounded, but sustained within a spiritual symmetry.

No one will ever completely understand or appreciate his or her Carmelite garden until eternity. At times it may be frightening inasmuch as it is a place of singular, ever-unfolding, terrible beauty. Yes, even in the summer tranquillity, thunderstorms can cause unexpected delight and horror. What will be revealed when spiritual lightning strikes one's soul? The inner landscapes change with the seasons of a person's days and years. The terrain is a ground of mystery, ever in transition. A pilgrim never knows what he or she will find. Beauteous foliage springs from seeds of self-sacrifice. Self-sacrifice originates from God's love within the heart and finds expression in love for others. As the sun rises and sets in the passing of time, so do the mysterious beauties in one's

Carmelite garden. To know the rose is to know a glimpse of the beauty of God. To know that the faded rose will bloom again is to have a glimpse of eternity. A pilgrim gazes long at cactus deserts, urban parks, pine forests, country meadows, fruited plains, rolling hills or rocky mountains. Each has a place in the garden of the soul. No matter where a person is on the road of life, he or she can wander in a garden. It is a place of retreat and repose. A Carmelite rests in the quiet and experiences prayer as ultimate mystery. In the peace of one's soul a pilgrim remembers people with restless, shallow or empty souls and nourishes them with silent prayer. Soul care is the most profound and essential concern for humanity. Carmelites vest themselves and their efforts into this phenomenon which will extend into eternity. It may rain or shine fiercely in one's Carmelite garden, but both are needed for it to survive and thrive.

A Nebulous Beauty

Love is the root of prayer and is in the essence of our consideration for those around us. This is especially true if their religious beliefs are different from ours. Quiet love speaks louder than most "holy" things we say, because it is manifest in the quality of our prayer and in our courtesy to others. We usually do not find quality prayer in excessive lengths of time spent in prayer; nor do we see quality concern in an excessive concern for others.

As Carmelites find that love takes on many expressions and blossoms in the strangest of ways, they learn to trust love. They do not look at periods of silence between God and themselves as negative or regressive. Silent areas in their inner selves are not awkward or disturbing, for in that silence something profound is happening that is beyond human comprehension. As it is shared with intimate friends, silence and love can be enriching and affirming in ways unknown. Quiet love quells the need to talk or understand.

Because those in Carmel do not know what expression love will take, it can surprise them at meetings, malls, parks, clinics or any other place. Since Carmel offers a way of living and loving that locates the good, true and beautiful in any environment, spiritual experiences can happen in the most unspiritual of places.

Carmelite practices are concrete ways by which to seek God. Mass, reflective prayer, the Liturgy of the Hours, Scripture study, Marian devotions and other daily or periodic exercises keep the members moving as they refine their spiritual values and ideals. Various practices foster and facilitate their journey toward union with God in an enriching and positive manner. Faithfulness to Carmelite practices remains intact as long as pilgrims keep their eyes and their hearts fixed on Jesus. If a particular practice becomes an end in itself, it may lead to false spiritual security or become an obsession. If pilgrims feel smug or satisfied about a certain practice, they lose their awareness of their constant need for God. They may even use a practice in a defensive way. If so, it becomes a barrier between themselves and God. Carmelites should keep their constant need for conversion paramount in their minds. The practices in Carmel should carry its members toward new insights. They can lose much of their value if members become preoccupied with them. Carmelite practices are a means to an end, the end of which is God.

Living the Carmelite rule and constitutions should enhance and never disrupt a person's daily responsibilities and obligations. A Carmelite way of life does not help a person to circulate in sophisticated or very holy coteries, make the proper religious connections, belong to prestigious prayer groups or give speeches about how often one engages in religious observances. Such notions only give glory to the self. Yes, the central focus of Carmel is prayer. However, there are no contests or other competitive events that evaluate who can pray the longest or the best, or who can do the most for God. True spirituality always turns Carmelites away from themselves and directs them toward God.

A sound Carmelite existence draws graces from spiritual practices and lets them silently seep into other areas of life. Everything becomes quietly spiritualized through this action, so that a harmonious balance can exist in prayer, family, work and leisure. Sanctity is found in the ordinary. To pray well one needs to sleep soundly, eat and exercise moderately, maintain care of his or her body and mind, facilitate supportive friendships, and work and play well. Self care becomes a holy occupation as a person sees addictions for what they are and do to individuals. Moving forward on the interior journey depends on a balance of external pursuits. Pilgrims recognize the centrality of God and the peripheral location of themselves. A peaceful, loving, selfless demeanor indicates the interior journey is going well because God transforms human hearts to an infinite extent. Humility can change a person from the inside out through prayer, virtuous living and honest love. There is no rest outside if there is no peace within an individual. Interior peace is the peace which allows Carmelites to live in peace with others. Pilgrims in Carmel journey with people and attempt to assist them in their efforts to pray and love, which are the major components of interior peace.

Carmelites are fully present to the world. They are in the world for the good of the world, but not of the world that pulls people away from God. They concentrate on God whom they seek and never completely find. As pilgrims, they pass through life and reach for the good to bring it to the fore. The unfathomable mysteries of grace, the infinity of God, the subtleties of his communications with them, and their own personalities give them ample opportunities to discover the good on this earth.

Many years well lived in the spirit of Carmel leads to an expanded perception and a deeper appreciation of reality. This happens through unexplained graces and might be compared with the talents of a virtuoso concert pianist which are present in a unique and highly commendable performance style. There is present concern for the music played. The performance is tuned to the time, place and receptivity of the people in the audience. The atmosphere of the concert hall and other variables change from performance to performance. One might say the concert pianist has a broad perspective regarding the pulse of the music and a heightened attentiveness to the total milieu. Indeed, many things are considered in a performance of which the audience is unaware. So it is with the quiet workings of grace.

With Thérèse of Lisieux, Carmelites are love at the heart of the Church. Instead of filling one's milieu with the sounds of music as the concert pianist does, the Carmelite fills it with the music of love and prayer. A noble call indeed, as love is a gift freely given. Each Carmelite gives these gifts in different ways, but always wraps them with the ribbons of prayer.

Carmelites are as diverse as the colors and hues in a spring garden. Whatever the color, the roots are deep in love at the heart of the Church. Carmel unceasingly opens people up to new ways in which they appreciate the fullness of love. Love expands hearts and the ability to welcome life as it comes. Pilgrims in Carmel find grace in the unexplained and give according to their talents and gifts. However, in their heart of hearts, their mission is to be as vessels of loving prayer.

Let us begin this wondrous journey. Pilgrims in Carmel need not be members of the Carmelite Order to live her charisms, grow in her lifelong beauty and wisdom, or climb her mountain. This holy mountain beckons all who desire a deeper union with God through Jesus Christ. Mary welcomes us, gives us a loving push forward and will be with us on our way. With the assurance of holy landmarks along the trail, we begin our journey up the mountain to the Triune God of ultimate mystery.

> Virgin Mary of Mount Carmel
> Whom in ancient prophecy
> God revealed to Saint Elias
> By an Oriental sea,

Rise again on God's creation,
Bring to bloom this arid place
With the white cloud of thy beauty
And the rainfall of thy grace.

Mother fair above all mothers,
By the Scapular we wear
By thy own Sign of Salvation,
Which our willing shoulders bear,
Shield us from the foes of darkness,
We are prey they seek to win.
Guard us as thy loving children
From the tragedy of sin.

Lady of the mystic mountain
Where the Lord has set His throne
Up its steep ways of the spirit
None can walk save love alone.
Grant us grace to climb Mount Carmel
And to learn that love is loss;
Guide us till our ways outdistance
All earth's treasures save the Cross.

Blessed Cloud of God's protection
And His luminous abode,
Light the pathway of thy pilgrim
To the Promised Land of God.
On the mount of contemplation
Be our surety and stay,
In the night a pillar glowing,
And a cloud of love by day.

Virgin of the Incarnation,
In the mysteries of grace
God has made His habitation
In our soul's most secret place.
Toward the height and inner kingdom

All our words and ways compel
For the Father, Son and Spirit
In its sacred silence dwell.

Queen and beauty of Mount Carmel,
Virgin of the solitude,
In the wilderness of Carmel
Lies the world's eternal good.
Draw us to its deep seclusion
And make God alone our goal
In the mystical Mount Carmel
That lies hidden in the soul.

Jessica Powers ["Virgin Mary of Mount Carmel," from *Proper of the Liturgy of the Hours* published by Institutum Carmelitanum, Rome, 1993. Reprinted by permission of Carmelite Monastery, Pewaukee, WI (copyright holder to Jessica Powers' poetry).]

2

Labors Along the Way

Nothing is more practical than finding God, than falling in love in a quite absolute, final way. What you are in love with, what seizes your imagination, will affect everything. It will decide what will get you out of bed in the morning, what you will do with your evening, how you spend your weekends, what you read, whom you know, what breaks your heart, and what amazes you with joy and gratitude. Fall in love, stay in love and it will decide everything.

Pedro Arrupe

Pope John Paul II tells us that work is a blessing from God. God created men and women to transform and rule the earth so that his work of creation may continue with their intelligence and effort.

There are many reasons why we work. Through our labor we try to produce something good and useful, or contribute something worthwhile, for ourselves and others. Our work is a way in which we connect with the world. We can create, help others, and put our knowledge and skills to good use. Work gives meaning and coherence to our lives. As long as it is for the betterment of humanity, it does not matter what we do, but how we do it. We do the best we can within the circumstances that shape our lives. Good work is God's love made visible, and one of the channels by which we learn and grow. A manager is threatened by new ideas and resists innovation which is indicated by the distance he maintains from his employees. He works because he has to in order to live, but fails to grow. A young mother sees each day as a new adventure. Her work gives life to her child and herself. She believes what she is doing really matters. The disposition we have toward our work has the capacity to deplete or sustain life. We cannot separate our spiritual lives and personal values from our work. What we do and how we do it is an expression of who we are as Christians. Carmel's spirit does not support idleness or inertia under the pretext of prayer or work. The balance and discipline of work has a primordial place in the life of Carmel because it helps counteract lackadaisical tendencies.

The service of work goes far beyond where we labor, or what we do to earn a salary. Work means anything we do that upgrades our lives: the many avenues of volunteer work, the tasks that maintain order and beauty in a home, our salaried jobs. Teresa notes: "What does it matter to us if we are serving in one way or another." As we do whatever our labors entail, we build up the world, each in our own way. Work keeps us in touch with reality, like an anchor that stabilizes our boat in the rough waters of life. It keeps us in the here and now, as we maintain our balance in the frustrations and insecurities, rewards and accomplishments that come with most of the jobs we do.

Our work supports our well-being in body, mind and spirit. There is an inherent value and beauty in sharing in the work of the world and doing our part for the kingdom of God on earth. We know no work or job is ideal, but learn to focus on what we like about our work. As we accomplish various tasks associated with our work, we feel positive about what we produce and put the small irritants and details we dislike in their proper place. We can make any job important by the way we define or view it.

Labor is partly enjoyable, partly disagreeable, but always inevitable. The great strides made in science and technology are awesome and fascinating. They also can demean and dehumanize us if we do not keep them in their right perspective. We live with many things we do not understand in our highly technical and computerized society. If we get overwhelmed or continually confused by the mysteries in our computers or other electrical gadgets in our homes or work we should dwell on the patron of a good life and a good death, Joseph of Nazareth. He lived with the most profound of mysteries, the incarnate Son of God and the Immaculate Virgin Mary, and did quite well. He can be the primary source of inspiration for those of us, especially neophytes, who use objects with much less mystery — computers. Joseph's life keeps everything we do not understand in its proper perspective, and makes the mysteries in computers seem like simple toys.

Joseph may tell us that it is the grace of God, working through the minds and hands of those who invent or discover things, which improves the quality of life and the degree of goodness in the world. However, Joseph would caution us not to be impressed by the largest, fastest, most powerful, latest or most expensive creations. A scaled down approach to that which is more manageable, less expensive and more compatible to the deeper needs of one's family is more practical to everyday life. Joseph guides us to serious responsibility regarding the short- and long-term effects of human intervention upon our natural resources, and the restrained and prudent use of energy. As a carpenter, Joseph respected the harmony and balance between God's natural gifts and human needs. We honor Joseph and his craft, as we keep careful watch regarding what we use and its effect on the delicate ecological balance of life in our world.

God created the world and then entrusted it to us so that we might continue creating through our love, care, wisdom and labor. Labor is an essential part of the rhythm of life. Indeed, the life of everyday routine work dedicated to God is hidden with Christ in God. For example, the labors of the kitchen helper, housekeeper, teacher's aide or laboratory technician may seem hidden and the work may be monotonous. However, a job well done, even though it goes unnoticed, may still provide the personal satisfaction of a job well done, thus exceeding that of so-called more important work. The young French Carmelite Thérèse of Lisieux wrote: "Draw profit from the smallest of deeds and do them for love.... Without love, deeds, even the most brilliant, count as nothing." The smallest of tasks are not done in vain if they are done for the love of God. For most of their years Jesus, Mary and Joseph lived a hidden life in a small town. That is something for deep thought. Our false pride rebels at dull routine and prefers accolades for spectacular accomplishments. Work can be a path to God if we do it for our family or others, in union with Jesus. However, it is so easy to jump off the path of humility and run down the trail of false pride. Our own glory may be enhanced by big money, lofty praise, important positions, or great rewards, but sooner or later all that comes to an end. Grace comes in many forms and quietly returns us to the path of humility.

Work activities flow more smoothly when they are focused in the heart and progress in a contemplative manner. The person who gives us the best example, and is above all other people honored as the ultimate example of the dignity of labor is, of course Joseph, the foster father of Jesus. He shows us how to work for our families, for our communities, for the common good and for the betterment of the world. However, he also reminds us that the positions we hold, projects we complete or tasks we accomplish are not our total identity as persons. We are greater and of more worth than what we do.

The dignity and value of work depends on the person who does it. Discipline gives work value because it is the essential tool for work. Without it nothing gets done. The love that we channel into our work is much more important than the social classification of the work we do. Dignity becomes a part of work when the people who perform it and their supervisors are responsible members of God's family. Employees take pride in doing their work well, with diligence and care. Employers seek to insure: honest communication, equal rights, sound safety rules for employees, safety checks on equipment, proper color and hue of the environment, good quality of light, circulation and temperature of air, availability of supplies and equipment, appropriate waste management and sound levels, design and support of furniture, pace of production, times and places for rest, fair and equal wages, health maintenance for employees and an openness to improvements in the workplace.

Faith joins our work with the redemptive work of Jesus. We unite with Jesus crucified as we endure the difficulties and hardships of our labor. Underneath our strengths and weaknesses, God's power is working in and through us. We rest in his power when automation replaces our skills, when nothing seems to go right, or when our material is poor or equipment inoperable. We accept what happens, do what we can, then step aside and let God take over. During our times under the shadow of the cross we find we are dispensable and things can go on without us. We rest in God's power as we take our reins of life, hand them over to Jesus and truly believe he is holding them. Because our work may change or no longer be necessary overnight, we take life as it comes. We are fully present to whatever task we do by doing it honestly, calmly, with consistency and a good sense of humor. This type of behavior during task performance says more about who we are than what we do. We are in the best of company when we hand over our reins of control to Jesus. During his time on the cross Jesus seemingly could not do or achieve anything. We feel that way sometimes. At that time his life seemed useless, but by being where he was he redeemed the world.

The Risks of Work

We may work toward a vision or dream and possess a strong belief that what we are doing really matters. As we do this, it helps to keep in mind the possibility that the work may become worthless or achieve no results. On the other hand, the results achieved may be opposite from what we expected. We should not put an extraordinary importance or be too dependent on the results of our labor. As we get used to this idea, we can concentrate on the values and goodness of the work itself rather than on the expected results.

Having so many things to do can create negative components that deteriorate our spiritual well-being. As an example, a middle-aged woman becomes more involved in doing good things for others. She accepts new responsibilities that come her way without discontinuing her old, unnecessary activities. She receives much praise for her labors, which increases her feeling of importance. She enjoys telling others about the good she is doing. The busier she is, the greater her feeling of self-importance becomes with frequent use of first person pronouns. Eventually the whirlwind of activities wears down her personal relationship with Jesus. Soon there is nothing more to give because the inner resources of the spiritual life have been depleted. The practical next step would be to realize what has happened and to give her reins of control over to Jesus.

Because it is popular in the society in which we live, the "oh so busy" trap is a very easy place in which to fall. The pursuit of a frenetic schedule may suggest several things. Praise from others meets a need for attention, approval or love that is not being met by inner resources or the people with whom an individual lives. The person may be unable to say no, or fear inactivity, solitude or his or her inner self. There may be long-standing problems that one does not want to define or confront, or an escape from serious thinking which needs to be done.

The more people involve themselves in many extraneous activities, the less they appreciate the finer details of life. This includes enrichment through different cultures, the many splendors of natural wonders and the beauty of really knowing people as unique individuals. Ultra busy people may desire rest and nothing to do for one or two weeks. However, when that time comes they may balk or be restless because they need involvement with people who ask them questions or seek their advice. Phones, fax machines, computers and personal contacts meet this need, but what are the reasons behind the need?

Being involved in too many things can keep us from serious thinking. If being busy with many things, even if they are good things, creeps into and predominates our daily existence, we should stop, look and listen with rigorous honesty. We face our time management problems after we dig below the surface dirt and look at the roots of what we are doing and why. Lamenting a problem dulls the edge of our emotions and focuses on the periphery of the problem. Defining a problem leads to the formulation of workable solutions and moves emphasis to the solution. A deep attentiveness views reconstruction of time problems from the roots up. There are several ways to uproot difficulties with time. A rigorous honesty with ourselves might suggest altering the hierarchy of things we do. We may modify what we do or how we do it, or eliminate picayune or lackadaisical activities. An evaluation or redevelopment of a practical, common sense orientation regarding use of our gifts and limitations may be worth a seasonal review.

We can easily become lost in our work. It is tangible, has boundaries, is usually satisfying and helps us feel worthwhile. We know work can hide or mask loneliness, deep seated problems, needed communication with others, conflicts within ourselves and prevent an authentic look at our inner journey to God. If work is taken too seriously, a compulsive or driven attitude may develop that extends into other areas of life. If that happens it is time to regroup and relax. Being too serious about work or taking too much time for it leaves too little time for playing, dreaming, goofing around, cultivating friendships, watching our children grow or taking opportunities for spiritual enrichment. A life balanced with work, play, study, time alone and with others, and prayer creates an openness to all that is beautiful. Such an orientation reaps unexpected blessings. We really can lead a fairly well-integrated life and accept the results whatever they may be without complications from work addiction.

The work ethic is embedded in our country's history. In any time period we find over-achievers and workaholics among all walks of life. Their achievements may be commendable but at what cost? All work is passing. Total concentration on work inhibits the experience of various joys in other areas of life and in life as a gift itself. Those who possess an inordinate attachment to their work may need more adjustment or help with events that alter their work schedules, such as a serious accident, plant closure, layoff, a debilitating injury or disease or retirement.

Our attitude toward chores can range from a pain in the neck to a pleasant experience. Most of us are accustomed to doing physical or mental activities directed toward the maintenance of ourselves, family and living environments. Many jobs are familiar and routine. Cleaning the kitchen, paying the bills, mowing the lawn, taking out the trash, washing the car or ironing the clothes are nothing to write home about but need to be done. Each person varies in the time, attention, effort and value he or she gives to each chore. If a child participates in family chores with a positive attitude, that attitude will most likely remain with him or her as an adult. Routine chores provide the opportunity for grumbles and complaints or fun and creativity. If we are comfortable with what we must do and like those with whom we work, chores may frequently be pleasing experiences and an avenue to holiness.

Stress in the workplace is common. The way we live and work, along with our attitudes and values, determine what is stress-ful to us and what is not. Stress may be positive or negative. It can motivate us to get a job done on time and help us to do something worthwhile we had thought was beyond our expectations. It can also wear us down, make us irritable or give us a sharp tongue. Stress can add to enthusiasm, excitement or energy that makes performing a task a positive experience, or deplete these attributes making the job a genuine depressant. One person views a particular stress as positive and another views it as negative. Most of the time stress can be positive, negative or a little of both. One person's enthusiasm or stimulation is another's anxiety or restraint.

Termination from a job is not stressful in the same way for all who experience it. Initially it can be devastating. After the initial shock wears off it may be a blessing in disguise that leads to better things. We can choose to mope and gripe or focus on what to do, then do it. We are not controlled by changes because we are neither victims nor slaves. Changes provide a new starting point based on the present moment in time. A response can range from minimal to maximal. We can make a choice, relying on God's graces and the actions of love in our lives. A time of pain is also a time of possibility. Various possibilities, provided by a seemingly negative event, can strengthen our resolve, test our resilience and inner resources, and inflame our creative spirit.

Thoreau said: "Money is not required to buy one necessity of the soul." That is true, and yet we need a source of income in order to sustain our lives while on earth. Money is not an evil in itself. It may become an evil by the way it is valued and used. We live in a highly consumer-oriented society where money is misused and abused. It can destroy or serve humankind. Money can buy the outer layers of many things but never the inner treasures within ourselves. It may purchase food but not appetite, medicine but not total health, acquaintances but not true friends, service but not faithfulness, times of joy but not interior peace. It is easy to see how, after the basic necessities of life have been met, money to spare directed to benefit others is of more value than money used to buy more things for ourselves. When the last hand is played and all the cards are on the table, the winner will find the treasure in the spiritual deck, not in the material one.

Elements of Labor

God rarely calls us to the comfort zone. The complexities of our communication systems, the downward pull from the effects of original sin, ruthless competition and other intervening variables, more often than not combine to make our place of work a place of teeth-gritting endurance.

Various signals may indicate trouble ahead in work situations. Something is awry if an individual frequently feels tense, stressed or driven during his or her work. Also, a person can feel tired after a day of work even though he or she was not over-worked. An easy going co-worker finds difficulty in getting along with others. An individual no longer feels comfortable with the work that has given years of satisfaction. A young man feels no motivation to participate in his favorite hobby. A caring individual suddenly gets caught up in the struggle for power and control. A woman near retirement uncharacteristically complains and wants to quit.

Any of these examples, if they last for a significant time period, should cause a person to stop, look and listen. It is time to face the issue, as there is no merit in ignoring or tolerating significant aberrations by letting them take their toll. A person should take immediate responsibility for, let us say, an excessive reaction to a minor disappointment or no reaction to the small pleasures of life. It is easier to face a problem when it happens than before it gets out of hand. To face the consequences of inappropriate reactions magnifies present difficulties and creates new ones.

Talking a problem through with a level-headed, truthful and trusted friend or professional relieves personal tension and presents the problem in a clearer light. Adding the basic ingredient of prayer will bring peace to mellow the situation. However, trusting ourselves and others takes courage. Trust involves taking responsibility, showing reliability and being accountable for our share of the labor within a common enterprise to which we are committed. As trusting individuals we desire truth but live in a world filled with lies and deceptions. Trust in others cannot be developed without a certain amount of risk. We face the possibility that our trust might be abused, betrayed or taken for granted. Yet we step forward in faith, since trust is the foundation on which sound relationships are built.

It takes time to do something well. The person who never makes a mistake either never does anything or lives without questions. If we did not make mistakes we would not be human. We can learn much from our mistakes and need not fear that the world will come to an end because of them. Our world will keep turning especially if the criticism we receive is constructive. Because constructive criticism is usually directed toward a specific action or behavior, our value as a person remains intact. An open mind will benefit from sound criticism. If criticism is destructive, we can try to take it with a grain of salt. Everyone is entitled to an opinion, whatever the opinion is. However, to compare ourselves with others regarding our positive or negative qualities wastes time and causes worry. When we no longer feel a person is a threat to us, that person probably will stop being a threat to us. In any event, friction is needed to polish and refine us because we know we are not perfect in most of the things we do. Realizing we have no control regarding how others see us, and that at times the workplace is neither fair nor just, helps us rest in the knowledge that positive outcomes may develop from disagreements and benefits from controversy.

Practical Application

There are little things we can do to make our lives easier. Often when we think of things to do and fail to write them down immediately, we may forget what it was we needed to do. A small log tablet on or near our person would help us in many ways. One page might be headed "Prayer" because this is the essence of our life with God. We take prayer requests seriously. We write down who we promise to pray for and why. If someone asks for our prayers because someone in their family is ill, and does not offer an update in a reasonable time, a gentle query might be made by the pray-er. Prayer requests should not be made in a light, haphazard or automatic fashion, or promised in a casual, nonchalant manner. A prayer is a gift from the heart and should not be treated superficially. Prayer is the most important communication in our lives. Another page could be headed "Phone." We write down the names and reasons for the calls we need to make. Just before our time for telephoning, we can arrange the names on the list according to their importance. A "To Do" page might follow and receives the tasks that need to be done immediately or within the week. A quick jot can save us from saying: "I should have done that." Writing things down on our log tablet helps us to remember and frees our minds to be more creative. Noting something we want to remember takes much less time and effort than trying to remember what we did not write down. Writing something down is taking the first step toward making it happen. When we write down ideas we discover other ideas and associations from those already written. Other titles for log tablet pages might be: Errands, Things to Read, People to Write, Fun Places to Go and Questions to Answer.

If we have too many tasks for the time available, we should ask ourselves which ones are the most important. We choose them and let go of the rest. We may ask someone else to do those tasks that, deep down inside, we know we will never get around to do. We also can let go of tasks that are not important or do not matter any more. If what we are doing is not above average on the satisfaction or reward scales, and is lengthy, tedious or repetitive, we can break it up into manageable time segments. After we finish a work segment we can treat ourselves. A treat need not be a sweet to eat, but rather a bit of play. A play treat at some point during a job, or after we complete it, helps us move ahead. It relaxes and diverts our attention with something enjoyable. A reference list of twenty fun things to do, each within a short period of time, would be worthwhile to construct and consult. It is advisable to make sure a fun activity is not another work task in masquerade. To reward work with work is defeat, even though one person's work is another person's play. Exercising, reading, shopping, or cooking can be work or play. Achieving through work remains in balance when the ability to play remains intact.

Paper management is critical in work simplification. A paper molehill can quickly become a mountain if we do not take action by replying to it, filing it or throwing it away. The daily mail may be sorted into task piles; then we respond to each pile. The junk mail finds a home in the refuse. Bills, letters, invitations or other mail requiring action may be placed in a "Do It This Month" box. Material for reading can be put at a place where it can be reviewed each month with a realistic attitude. Although promotional advertisements can be enticing, we subscribe to literature for which we have time to read and keep what really interests us.

A large calendar placed near the phone will help us formulate our days. We record external appointments from visiting the doctor to getting the car serviced. Internal appointments such as writing a proposal or recording various deadlines may appear, hand in hand, with happy events such as lunch in a park, a tennis game or a trip to the mountains.

Spiritual events need to be noted too, as they keep us in touch with the future. A good size calendar close at hand saves time and energy. Overly busy people can down scale their activities by letting blank spaces remain blank. An uncluttered calendar reflects an uncluttered mind. The compulsively busy person can draw lines through a few days in the month. These lines are a sign that this is special time to spend as one wants. Unplanned time is a good balance and allows for the unexpected. It also decreases the pressure of things to do.

When we work on a project the first step toward completion

is to research and brainstorm. A car wash or bake sale without publicity before the event is doomed to failure. An individual who plunges into a project before he or she thinks it through and anticipates possible problems makes project implementation difficult. Most of us know the value of presenting spontaneous ideas, thoughts and musings before we start actual work on a project. Looking at the many small and large parts of a project and isolating them into manageable portions is especially helpful if the project sounds overwhelming or intimidating. Viewing small parts of a project that can be accomplished in a realistic and practical manner makes completion of the total project more attainable.

Anything we need, or need to do, may be seen as a goal, from cleaning the attic to taking a trip, to earning a post graduate degree. The development of a positive goal comes from a need to change things for the better. If our goal is to exercise regularly, we can list our assets and limits regarding age and health, check with our physician and learn about exercise programs and facilities. We can visit places, talk to people and choose what is best for us. We might even formulate goals within a goal, such as increasing the strength of specific muscle groups, improving endurance or decreasing weight at a reasonable rate. Our achievement of projects within a goal is a strong incentive to continue with the main goal.

Success in completing projects or tasks depends on a clear vision of one's strengths and weaknesses. People are usually night owls or skylarks. The owls experience their highest energy and most creative times at night, and the larks in the morning. Low energy times can be used for routine tasks and activities that do not need much cognition. The best time to do quality work is during high energy periods. Self-discipline gives us time to think about what we do and how we do it. We might list our daily activities, and note the amount of time and effort we put into each task. Energy is conserved and work is simplified when time is managed well and work is accomplished with organization and precision. We maintain flexibility when the art of delegation is put into practice.

We finish one task before we go on to the next one, and, unless there is an emergency, rarely do anybody else's job.

When we work we concentrate on the task at hand. Time spent thinking about a vague something that might happen, a better job, what we are going to do on our day off or on vacation or imagining conversations are distracting. Uncommon wishful thinking depletes energy, limits attention and decreases the satisfaction we find in the daily mastery of the task at hand. To frequently view work as a stepping stone to some future event defeats the value, enjoyment and respect the present moment contains. These three attributes challenge us to keep our minds and hearts where we are physically. We work to the best of our abilities in the sacrament of the present, in the presence of God.

Usually, the more we care for the work we do the closer we come to God. We strive to work with patience and perseverance and by that give honor to the work process and product. All work is equal when we really care for what we do. Writing a book is no more special or better than mopping the floor. We do not work to "find ourselves" or compete with others. When we work with care we give of ourselves and realize our interdependence with others. The beauty of the process and product of work enriches us and gives integrity to what we do. The final products encourage us to move forward. Usually things can be done better. Our potential will never be fully realized on our earthly journey. To enjoy each step during our work is our achievement and accomplishment. To rush to complete a task in order to rush to something else is to miss the point. For what are we rushing? The flowers of interior peace do not grow among the weeds of poorly regulated daily activities or a fast, fragmented life. We manifest a radiance and serenity as we rest in God internally and use discipline in our conduct externally. We build new strength as we perform our tasks with attention and limit ourselves to a few well-chosen activities each day. Often we know our best is not the absolute best, but we relax and trust that things will work out without our being perfect or totally in charge. By letting others help us, we accept their gifts and join forces with them as their talents and experiences come to the fore. Working together with others provides a connection and unity with humanity that is enriching, life-giving and exceptionally beautiful.

A greater good permeates our minds as we change and grow. We unite with God's will as we strive to respond with trust and love to every situation in which we find ourselves. The will of God requires a continual search for truth and a constant effort to open ourselves to greater love. The way we love affects the rest of the world. As we strive to grow in God by working for the betterment of his world, our spiritual development teaches us that true spirituality is not a part of the secular world because it is not a consumer product. It cannot be bought or sold. While many people have lost their sense of the supernatural, many more are searching for it. To seek God's will is to lay down our lives in surrender and emptiness because God works in our brokenness. Becoming closer to God makes us more sensitive to what is going on within and around us. God helps us to find our inner still point so that we can focus and respond to the less tangible things in life. Faith is not based on our intellectual convictions, interior feelings or philosophical ideas. Faith, as an intangible force, helps us hang on no matter what and reach out to others in their need.

Life in Carmel is a prayerful presence. Carmelites, especially secular Carmelites, can permeate with good the many seen or unseen evils in the work place — or any other place, for that matter. A Carmelite's first line of defense is prayer. A prayer warrior, armed with quiet prayer, can be effective almost anywhere. Not a word needs to be said. As Carmelites we manifest a prayerful presence by how we conduct ourselves during times of crises and uncommon stress, and how we behave on days that are dull and drab or dark and stormy. A Christlike presence among spiritually illiterate people can do more for them than can be imagined. Carmelites look for Christ in each person and focus on that which is positive without being naive. Naivete is not a virtue nor evil an abstraction. To live Carmel is to work with God's creative powers as we use our talents and skills with hope and enthusiasm. Work becomes a channel through which God's presence and generating love flows into the environment. All work blessed by God is an expression of his ongoing creative concerns. Prayer holds work and the world together in the sacred presence of God. Work gives Carmelite pilgrims the opportunity to find God who may be hidden in small errands or Herculean projects. From time to time, work becomes a wordless lead into prayer as hands and minds are kept to the work and hearts are rapt in God. Work is a blessing and sacrifice in joy and sorrow that is offered to God for the building up of his kingdom on earth.

Carmelites know that the most integrated person is not the one who does the most, but rather the one who gives the most. The gift of self goes beyond talents or skills to a loving awareness of a life in Christ. Whatever a Carmelite does should come from the heart and deepen integrity, self-knowledge, and the capacity to love. Indeed, work is a place where love unfolds.

In the Middle Ages three workers were asked what were they doing. One man said he was cutting ridiculous boulders with outdated tools and putting them together like the supervisor said. He was cursing the blazing sun and his back was killing him. The second worker noted that he was shaping boulders into functional forms which were to be assembled by others. He worked hard. It was repetitive labor, but he was earning a salary and supporting his family. The third worker simply raised his eyes to heaven and said with a radiant smile: "I'm building a cathedral!"

We too can make this world a more beautiful and loving place. As we walk through our days we make decisions. Our mature decisions reflect a refined moral dimension and a quiet concern for those who suffer from injustice. Decisions are rarely black or white, but frequently the result of discussing priorities and choosing what is best. Each choice, no matter how insignificant, teaches us about ourselves and expresses our loyalties. In our present time, even traffic congestion calls for a choice. Some may grumble, others may say a rosary. If we experience trouble, it really is not the difficult event that counts; rather it is how we comprehend and respond to it. Like the third man answered, may we help build a few cathedrals in our lives.

John of the Cross encourages us. He said: "In all things, both high and low, let God be your goal, for in no other way will you grow in merit and perfection." If our primary occupation is loving God, that love will bless and permeate everything we do. John gives us a beautiful description of his love in this poem:

> My beloved is my bridegroom
> And my Lord — O what a joy!
> I will henceforth all the powers
> Of my soul for him employ;
> And the flock that once I tended,
> Now I tend not as before
> For my only occupation
> Is to love him more and more.
>
> I have gone away forever
> From the haunts of idle men
> And a sharer in their follies
> I will never be again.
> They may say, and say it loudly,
> I am lost, but I am not;
> I was found by my beloved,
> O how blessed is my lot.

3

Food for the Journey

> The Blessed Eucharist, therefore, is the very heart of
> Christianity since it contains Christ himself and since it
> is the chief means by which Christ mysteriously unites the
> faithful to himself in one body. *Thomas Merton*

A Carmelite missionary was walking in an African jungle when
he heard the ominous plodding of a lion behind him. "Oh Lord,"
prayed the missionary, "Grant in Thy goodness that the lion
behind me is a good Christian lion." In the silence that followed
the missionary heard the lion praying: "Bless us O Lord and these
Thy gifts which we are about to receive...."

Nourishment is a genuine necessity while traveling on our
spiritual journey. The Eucharistic banquet is our most important
bread of life and our primary source of spiritual sustenance. This
greatest mystery of our faith is our essential reality. The person of
Christ is the fullness of the Eucharistic mystery, and the greatest
mystery of love. God, the infinite, humbled himself to the point of
disappearing under the appearance of bread. Transubstantiation is
the complete change of the substance of bread and wine into the
substance of Christ's body and blood. Jesus, his whole being and
his divine nature, is with us as gift. His real presence draws each
of us deeper into union with God and union with each other.

The Eucharist, as sacrifice and banquet, has great power
to transform us and the way we do things. Jesus graced a meal
by bestowing it with the highest of honors. The celebration of

the Eucharist is the greatest sacrifice and the most sacred meal of God's family, the Church. As food, the Eucharist spiritually nourishes us and makes us one with the risen Christ.

We partake of the bread of life with reverence and strive to become one in the body of Christ with love. Holy communion gives us strength to be better Christians. The Eucharist is the food we need more than ever in this age of fragmentation and unrest. It is the point of greatest unity, as our bodies and souls become one with Christ.

As we reflect on the vast importance of the Eucharist, we can discover ways to improve and enrich our personal eating habits. The staff of life for our souls leads us to prudent reflections about the staff of life for our bodies. A major concern for Teresa was that her Carmelites have common sense. If a soul is to thrive, it needs a nourished body in which to reside. Prayer concentration is limited when a person has a full or empty stomach, or if he or she has been inordinately fasting, binge eating or extensively feasting for a significant period of time. Because what one eats has a direct relationship with one's spiritual journey, Teresa advises that meals for Carmelites usually be plain, nourishing, simply prepared and eaten in moderation.

Food as Stress

As we share food with others at the same table, we get to know them better on the natural level. We share food that becomes part of our bodies and a reason for fellowship. A pleasant and supportive association of people united in faith can be likened to the breaking of bread together. The beauty and importance of dining with others has lost its significance in our society today because the gobble syndrome is so prevalent. We often eat meals alone, in haste or on the run, even eating in cars or other modes of transport as we travel from one place to another. Fast food enterprises and business lunches are hallmarks of our time. Combining eating with another activity is becoming the norm. Encouraging the custom of breaking bread together would have a positive effect on eating habits and our relationships with each other.

How we eat might resemble a barometer which measures how we feel about our life at the present time. A gnawing loneliness, interior emptiness, subliminal anxiety or significant boredom may be felt in the pit of the stomach. We may feel hungry but do not know what we want to eat. A need for security, reassurance, love or acceptance may be temporarily met by automatic eating. For a short time we feel better, but like a prostitute's or gigolo's caresses, this short term substitute soon leaves us emptier than ever. We again feel alone, anxious or bored. It would be good to remember that we eat to satisfy hunger, not to change how we feel.

One of the things of which we should be aware is the various ways stress can be present when we eat. The first step in reducing food stress is to acknowledge what kind of stresses are present and how we currently experience them.

Food stress is most commonly caused by being pulled in other directions as we eat. For instance, eating and driving are two tasks and maybe three if our mind is focusing on what we need to do when we reach our destination. To take meals with loud noises present can also be unsettling. Eating with the TV news can reverse digestion and agitate or numb the mind. Combining meals with important business meetings, evaluation sessions or other work usually causes the gastronomic tract to work harder. Eating in this manner involves body and mind activities that are not conducive to sound digestion. Speed eating for any reason increases the risk of choking and other unpleasantries. It also limits the time necessary to taste, savor and fully enjoy meals.

Like intoxicants, eating can become an addiction. Eating may be a way of coping with fear, stress, emotional discomfort or avoiding painful areas in our lives. Food, too, can be used to avoid problems. We can get over-involved or fixated on the aspects of food selection, preparation, presentation and consumption. Baking or cooking can be an automatic response to feelings of discomfort or depression. Eating can be a crutch to help us through times when we cannot cope. We can have many comfort foods of which we automatically consume. However, using food for comfort or solace can become insidiously destructive.

We live in a developed country and our relationship with food is very complex. Nature is often manipulated to meet our needs. Most of us live physically and psychologically far from where the growth and production of food takes place. Many of us would become vegetarians if we had to kill the animals we eat or study how they live. The average person spends little time thinking about what goes on inside slaughterhouses or wondering where they are located. Many animals we eat are raised on industrialized factory farms with emphasis on high profit rather than on traditional family farms that consider the well-being of the animals.

We must eat in order to live physically, yet psychologically some of us live in order to eat. Our preoccupation with food may have little to do with our actual hunger. Most of the time it is possible to get the food we want in any season, thanks to modern transportation. Many of us buy groceries in mega-markets that resemble absolute cornucopias of food. We are baffled by the thousands of items from which to choose, are prompted to buy food we do not really need and discover foods that were not around a few years ago. Most of us are no longer occupied with the sorrows and joys that come from raising our own food. All we need is the money to purchase it.

Our massive food production and distribution systems illustrate our collective interdependence and interconnections. Yet we tend not to think of the effects of a nationwide strike by those who drive the specialized transports that supply our local stores with food. Another area of food stress is diseases that relate to our affluence, our abundance and our over-consumption of food in general and passion for certain foods in particular. Residues from fertilizers and pesticides, and additives and preservatives used by the food industry are relatively new to our biochemical physiology. We do not know what long-term exposure to some of these residues and food chemicals will lead to in future generations. If we truly are what we eat, we need to pay attention to everything we put into our bodies in a sensible, non-alarmist, non-fanatical way. Those on a "see-food" diet eat everything they see. They do not consume edibles because of an exotic compulsion, they just lack the self-discipline of will power. Most of us overindulge from time to time, but to do this frequently leads to serious self-destruction. A change in diet that promotes health and prevents or slows disease must be undertaken with a serious commitment that comes from intelligence, rather than anxiety or paranoia. We become more aware of our relationship with food when we realize our automatic behavior concerning what we eat. Let us reflect on our thoughts, feelings and social customs regarding poor food choices and the amount we eat. What are the underlying motives, impulses and behavior that support our poor eating habits?

The eat and run approach to meals is common in our society; it is an approach that can be changed. We can regain the ability to enjoy the simple pleasures found in dining together. Does our kitchen resemble a cafeteria or fast food eatery? The most popular room in a home is the kitchen. A clean, well-stocked, pleasantly decorated, organized kitchen with counter space and appropriate appliances is an ideal that most of the time will encourage us to do kitchen tasks. A cluttered, disorganized, dirty kitchen with minimal supplies and broken appliances will have the opposite effect. Kitchens can be comforting, pleasant, distasteful or repelling. The people, objects and events in our kitchen must not be bland enough to cause lethargy nor unduly hectic to cause conflict. Our kitchen makes a statement about our values, interests, identity and lifestyle and may be viewed as the heart room of a home. This is the room in which we can live, work and play and experience dark nights and spiritual lights. Its milieu should compliment our skills and competence. This popular room reflects the attitudes of the people who use it and influences how they work in it. A kitchen is a good place to learn family responsibility which includes: cleaning up one's own messes, putting away what one uses, opening things and closing them, moving things and putting them back, writing items on the shopping list that one has used up and finishing liquids so that a few drops do not remain for the next person.

Food as Sacred

Eating is one of the most enjoyable pleasantries of life. In the gospels Jesus often shared a meal with others. Jesus ate with sinners to show his forgiveness and to bring them peace. We are sinners who eat with sinners and are created to forgive ourselves and others and restore peace. As we gather to share the same food we also join in mutual sharing, support and unity. How pleasant our shared meals would be if we kept these thoughts in our hearts. Peaceful conversation is so important, especially during mealtimes. Effort, energy and love go into buying food, preparing and serving it, attending to the physical and social environment in which we dine and cleaning up afterwards. Work becomes lighter when each member of the household is responsible for something concerning the meal. Indeed, cooperation bolsters unity and peace.

A sound sense of conviction and purpose, as well as knowledge of the love others have for us, aids us to eat for the right reasons. Eating nourishing foods brings a sense of delight because we are partaking of gifts from God's love, and we share his love when we share our food with others.

There is an old story that tells of a man who lived a long and worthy life. When he died, the Lord said to him: "Come, I will show you hell." He was taken to a room where a group of people sat around a round table, in the middle of which was a huge pot of stew. Each person had a spoon that reached the pot, but the handle was so long it could not be used to reach their mouths. Everyone felt starved and desperate. The suffering was horrible. After awhile the Lord said: "Come, now I will show you heaven." They came to another room. To the man's surprise, it was identical to the first room. A group of people sat around a round table with a pot of stew in the center. Again, each held the same long handled spoon. However, here everyone felt nourished and happy. The room was full of laughter and joy. "I do not understand," said the man. "Everything is the same, yet they are so happy here. They were so miserable in the first room. What is going on?" The Lord smiled, "Ah, but do you not see? Here they have learned to feed each other."

We feed each other in more ways than we realize. Eating with others gives us opportunities for self-denial and times to express appreciation. Honest gratitude may be extended for the food itself, and for the events and people that were responsible for bringing it to us. We remember the sun and rain, seeds and plants, planters, pickers and packers, transporters and sellers. Finding a sense of the sacred in how the food becomes part of us as it becomes our blood, tissue, organs and their proper functioning, unites body and soul. A sense of the sacred is in life and in death. When the soul, the force of life, breaks free from the body, the physical body disintegrates, and with the passage of time, returns to the elements of the earth that will nourish new life. All these thoughts should increase our respect for food. We use what we need and give the rest away. Careful selection of the food we eat and minimal waste helps us to be ecologically responsible. Hungry people are near and far. Our work for better global distribution of resources gives peace to our heart and soul.

Small shared meals that begin with a blessing and continue with light and happy conversation can be meals of great worth. Large meals with tensions that rise from conflicts or problem solving endeavors can be meals of endurance. Meals are not the place to discuss overwhelming problems, family trials and tribulations or other serious matters that might evoke heated arguments. As we put aside the work concerns of the day and enjoy eating and being together, we form a greater appreciation of the present moment. Our minds need not wander to past or future activities.

As we eat a peach in the present moment we might first look at the beauty of its color, shape and size. Next we might feel its texture and smell its fragrance. What thoughts come to mind during these different sensory perceptions? When we are ready to take the first bite we might notice how we are holding the peach in our hand. The movement of our hand to mouth and the first bite with taste of skin and fruit may bring forth new observations. We chew and taste and chew and taste again until the fruity flesh changes to pulp and liquid. When we eat in this manner one bite of peach can be immensely satisfying. We swallow one bite, and perhaps follow it with a "mmmmm," before we take the next bite. Eating a peach can be a contemplative experience when we do it slowly and give thought to what is really happening to the food. Perhaps we might not think but just feel. This would eliminate major likes and dislikes, and other judgments. We learn to enjoy food by adding lightsome fun or spontaneously sharing food with others. We also know not to keep too tight or too loose a hold on the pleasantries of eating. The relaxed grasp is open to the joy of serendipity. The peach pit may even evoke a sense of wonder as we look at it closely. When we eat attentively we know that the simplest of foods, or recipes, can make the finest of meals.

During a meal a silent awareness of our eating and drinking will alert us to whether or not we are consuming too much or too little. When we leave the table while still somewhat hungry we may experience a sense of solidarity with those who are hungry in our world. Sometimes, we may hunger for the kingdom of God. These thoughts assist in our process of spiritual formation. We know the danger of not eating and of eating large meals quickly.

We know eating several small meals a day is more healthful to body, mind and soul than eating a few large meals. We cannot go wrong when we eat a variety of good foods in moderation. As we eat we rotate the foods as this helps us enjoy the different tastes more than eating one food until we finish it. As we progress in the area of wise eating a desire for natural whole foods develops and meals that contain fresh fruits and vegetables and whole grains takes precedence over most other meals most of the time. We are more conscious of the quality of the food we eat, how it was grown or made, what is in it and from where it came. We recognize our attachments or cravings for particular foods and also realize how strongly our social and cultural orientation influence our dietary habits. We are well schooled in what foods energize or tire us, or make our bodies feel light or heavy. After significant research we find where we can get unbiased, reliable information about food and nutrition. We appreciate the value of water and drink it instead of popular drinks or diet colas. We cast a cynical glance upon the credibility of fad diets. When we shop it becomes a practice to read food labels to note fat, salt and sugar content and other nutritional information. We review our favorite recipes and make alternations to minimize health defeating ingredients.

Our attention focuses on our inner journey, noting that kindness to others and acceptance of ourselves, rather than societal norms, dictate what is physically attractive. We know that true beauty radiates from the soul and becomes richer and deeper in time and with grace on our spiritual journey.

The Guest Unseen

Brother Lawrence was a seventeenth century lay brother at the Monastery of Discalced Carmelite Friars in Paris. Formerly a soldier, he had a natural aversion to anything in the kitchen. However, during the fifteen years he worked in the monastery kitchen, he became skilled in the culinary arts and found his route to sanctity. What was his secret? He accustomed himself to doing everything there for the love of God and asked God for the grace to do the work well. God uses unexpected things like pots and pans and even kitchen sinks, to bring us close to him.

Sharing a meal can be a very spiritual experience. Quiet meals, without radio, TV or stereo interference, enhance the sacred quality of eating. Jesus revealed himself during meals in many places in the New Testament. We know them well: the miracle of the loaves and fishes; eating with a tax collector; the breaking of the bread on the road to Emmaus; and a breakfast of fish and bread on the shore of the Sea of Tiberias. However, the most unforgettable of all meals was the Last Supper. Thomas Aquinas wrote: "O sacred banquet in which Christ becomes our food, the memory of his passion is celebrated, the soul is filled with grace, and a pledge of future glory is given to us."

Spiritual nutrition at meals begins with an appropriate prayer. We pray for those who helped in preparing the food and for those who are about to eat it. Migrant farm workers, wholesale buyers and innumerable others depend on the food industry for jobs. All who work with and eat food have souls. We do not know who among them are in need of prayer. We can remember them before we partake of the fruit of their labors. Prayers while cooking aid in food preparation and thanksgiving prayers show our gratitude to God for his bounty.

When Thomas Merton entered the monastery, his abbot gave him and his postulant companion a few words of advice. Each one would make the community either better or worse. Everything the postulants did would have some influence on others that would either be positive or negative; and so it is with us. We influence those with whom we live, work and eat. We may or may not be aware of this reality. Note a family at the dinner table and observe the positive and negative directions in their behavior and conversation. Dining with good manners, proper etiquette, and a courteous and respectful demeanor with gentle, pleasant communication refines a meal with grace, dignity and charm. Perhaps listening to a spiritual tape or soft classical music might be in order. To consume our food in a leisurely, calm and relaxed manner does much good for the body, mind and soul. Proper digestion results in physical benefits, as well as social and spiritual enhancement.

How lovely it would be to use the rich and vast liturgical calendar of the Church when we plan our meals. The ever-changing seasons and saints days can be remembered at our meals and brighten them up with color and new bits of knowledge. Place mats and napkins may reflect the color of the liturgical season or saint, and make the main meal a celebration of God's love and goodness to us. Food and centerpieces can reflect the country in which a family member's name day saint was born or served. Suitable holy cards or simple Christian quotations at each person's place brings our splendid liturgical cycle home to us in a personal way. Our liturgical calendar gives us endless opportunities to be creative and imaginative when we celebrate its saints and seasons.

Jesus is the unseen guest at our table. He helps us enjoy the simple pleasures found in taking food together and enhances our fellowship and mutual respect for each other. As we eat and talk with care and thankfulness, in a leisurely fashion, we bond in unity with Jesus and each other. We see his presence in each person and grow in his life and love. With Jesus, meals bring a joy that is far beyond current feelings or emotions. Our joy touches our lives at its deepest center where God dwells within us. Joy is the by-product of God's love for us, and our love for him. Our greatest change occurs as we become more Christ-like through Holy Communion. In a lesser context the common food we eat becomes a part of us. We are part of a great circle of events. Our physical nourishment comes to us through the earth, sun, rain, plants and animals. This is quite awesome and echoes the words of Genesis: "And God saw all that he had made and it was good." We find God's grandeur in a drop of rain, a ray of sun and everything that helps food grow.

He is found in the meager meal and the great celebration of the Eucharist. Because companionship around the dinner table has many sacred qualities, perhaps at the end of a good meal we can take some quiet time to reflect upon these words of grace:

> Oh Thou who clothest the lilies
> And feedest the birds of the sky.
> Who leadest the lambs to the pasture
> And the hart to the waterside.
> Who dost multiplied loaves and fishes
> And converted water into wine.
> Do Thou come to our table
> As guest and giver to dine.

4

Desert Lands

We shall steer safely through every storm so long as our heart is right, our intention fervent, our courage steadfast and our trust fixed on God. *Francis de Sales*

A desert is a frightful place. Yet, it must be traversed for it is part of the terrain of the Carmelite soul. Many who live the charisms of Carmel would rather journey around the external boundaries of this barren land, for its stark light reveals interior realities we would prefer not to see. However, with trust in God, we meet and learn the blinding truths at the heart of this land of blazing heat and bright light.

In the forays of beginnings, wanderings around the desert's edge seem like high noons in our spiritual lives. Our souls are laid bare as we find how we unconsciously compromise our values to those the secular world promotes. Subtle and not so subtle media advertisements affect and infect us in ways of which we are unaware. We direct more energy to looking good, getting ahead and being liked than to what a simple Christian life requires. The strong desert light within probes our hearts and reveals the corrosion of secularism and its consequent effect on our relationship with God. It is most difficult to live in the secular world and not become polluted by its false values. The harsh desert is most helpful as its blazing light reveals camouflaged and hidden evils and motivates us in our relentless search for truth.

The desert uncovers how often we evade our true selves.

Our involvement with others may prevent knowledge of self. The things for which we blame and fault others may be what is unacceptable in ourselves or prevents their discovery in ourselves. If others cause most of our faults, we would have little opportunity to grow. Our efforts to help others in need may be laudable in the eyes of others, but for whom do we really do them? We may change our good activities to remain in accord with popular ministries, current thinking, or our own need to receive love. We may have a true desire to be of service or a strong need for self-esteem. Our external projection of virtue and holiness may be muddied by internal negatives or a critical attitude. The searing desert sun burns away our self-built fortifications and exposes harsh inner truths. It is easy to project our own evils or needs on others. Desert wisdom shows us the importance of taking responsibility for the reasons behind our actions and mistakes. A clear vision lets us see that many things that are wrong in the world are the same things that are wrong within ourselves.

As we progress through the dry, unknown landscapes in the desert, fear seems to be our constant companion. In the deserts of our souls the dark secrets and hidden lusts that we may have been harboring are laid bare. Confronting them fills us with fear. Yet, with God's grace, we find the courage to do so and, as a result, learn to become more tolerant of and compassionate for the weaknesses we see in others.

The solitude of the desert provides no place to run or hide. Previously unfaced addictions and resentments may raise their heads. The glare of the desert exposes the startling truth that there is no lasting security or lasting comfort in this world. As the dark shadows of our desert night lighten with God's grace, we come to terms with our own powerlessness and vulnerabilities. We no longer feel driven to solve everyone's problems or feel called to save the world. We note that God works in his good time. Our projects, plans, ideas and activities are of less importance than we thought. The urgencies of life take their appropriate place in the reality of life when God is truly at the center of our life. Yes, we learn from what we experience. The more we face ourselves honestly and directly the more our hearts expand and open to God. In the desert we are stripped to the basics of life and prayer and feel starkly alone. There are no televisions, phones, videos, computers, favorite arguments or theological disputes. God and the spiritual life are void of our complexities. The desert lands are where we seek God and where we alone can find him.

We may entertain thoughts that the desert is an extraordinary spiritual place and we are extraordinary spiritual people because we are within it. Such thoughts result from spiritual fantasies that animate the spiritual ego. Such ideations are nonsense since most deserts take place in our kitchen, bedroom or workplace. The real desert encourages us to be our authentic selves and discourages any inclination toward putting on a holy act.

Prayer in the desert is quiet and unnerving. There are no supports, no sweet sentiments, no warm feelings. In desert prayer we hide nothing and surrender ourselves to God's mercy. We remain faithful in the vast unknown. The unpleasant realities we find in ourselves serve to remind us to do better and to remember God is with us. During these times he is more present to us than we are to ourselves. The words of John of the Cross burn in our souls: "I will take you by a way you know not to the secret chamber of love." God loves us with a love we cannot imagine or comprehend. The answers we wish to so ardently find in life may not come. We consider how often life resembles walking through a sand storm in the desert. Blessed are we who are poor enough to live without the satisfaction of clear or even partial answers.

In the Shadows of Pain

Every individual is unique in many ways. One way is in how a person experiences and interprets pain. Fear of getting hurt may cause a person to shy away from relationships and activities. When an individual overcomes this specific fear, anticipation about relationships and activities may be less painful and even pleasant.

Pain is subjective. We may experience a common cold as a minor nuisance, advanced pneumonia, or a sign of imminent death. Our desert times help us keep things in proper perspective. Society states: Pain is the enemy, it is of no value and we must find relief at all costs. Quick treatment may alleviate the pain but, what if a patient stays with the pain for awhile and tries to find what it is saying? This may lead to deeper revelations that suggest there is need to face, examine, and reform particular areas in one's life. Perhaps their complaints are symptoms of some kind of mental or spiritual dysfunction.

Pain is an inevitable part of life. What we do with it can make all the difference in our lives. We may deny pain, make it the center of our lives, reject it as an enemy, accept it as a teacher, fight it or work around it. Frequently we can try to accept it as friend and teacher. Pain can expose and test us in ways unimaginable. With God's help we emerge with greater strength of character, better endurance, and greater hope. The true meaning of life stands out more clearly as pain purges us from pretense, callousness and a multitude of vanities.

A hallmark of our humanness and mortality is suffering. It requires respect when appropriate treatment cannot alleviate it. Time teaches us that suffering need not victimize or control us. The energy we use to fight, flee or forget a specific pain can be redirected to a greater good. The transformation of pain expresses itself in an inner joy that aids in prayer, in the salvation of souls and in ministry to others. We can work around our pain and discover new interests or talents more beautiful than anything we knew about or had before the pain. We may be healed at a deeper level even though not cured of the pain. After we receive a diagnosis and assimilate information about it, we work toward reasonable independence and do not resist, defy, escape, trivialize or aggrandize our condition. We take a great step forward when we look into the face of our pain and see the face of God. However, that takes time and some doing. Teresa supports us with a truth of the desert: "The greatest honor God can grant a soul is not to give much to it, but to ask much of it."

The desert teaches us that suffering can bring out the best as well as the worst in us. We invite needless suffering when we exaggerate our own suffering or give more attention to it than is necessary. An unknown author wrote: "Today, upon a bus, I saw a lovely girl with golden hair. I envied her, she seemed so gay and wished I were as fair. When suddenly she rose to leave, I saw her hobble down the aisle. She had one leg and wore a crutch. But as she passed, a smile! Oh, God forgive me when I whine, I have two legs. The world is mine! I stopped to buy some candy. The lad who sold it had such charm. I talked with him. He seemed so glad. If I were late 'twould do no harm. And as I left he said to me, 'I thank you. You have been so kind. It's nice to talk with folks like you. You see,' he said, 'I'm blind.' Oh, God forgive me when I whine, I have two eyes. The world is mine. Later, while walking down the street, I saw a child with eyes of blue. He stood and watched the others play. He knew not what to do. I stopped a moment, and then I realized he could not hear. Oh, God forgive me when I whine, I have two ears. The world is mine. With feet to take me where I'd go, with eyes to see the sunset's glow. With ears to hear what I would know. Oh, God forgive me when I whine. I'm blessed indeed. The world is mine."

Suffering brings people together. It strips them down to a basic level where they know themselves and others better through the wisdom of their wounds. Suffering transforms and sanctifies us when we unite it with the crucifixion of Jesus. When Jesus died the excess of evil was mastered by the excess of love. Everyone who truly accepts Jesus as God accepts Jesus through the cross. The cross is the meeting point of hate with love and evil with good. John of the Cross wrote: "And I saw the river over which every soul must pass to reach the kingdom of heaven, and the name of that river was suffering. And I saw the boat which carries souls across the river, and the name of that boat was love."

Love and compassion grow from the seeds of redemptive suffering. We share in the redemptive work of Christ by uniting our suffering and the suffering of others with Jesus. We share in the pain of others as we give them strength and try to decrease their sorrow. As we share with others in pain we strengthen the body of Christ at its weakest points. The deeper we try to fathom the mystery of redemptive suffering, the more effective we will be in genuinely caring for others.

If we know someone who is poor, chronically ill or living alone we may long to give them money, alleviate their pain or find them a companion. We begin at once to make plans that will help fix things and are stimulated to give verbal expression to our ideas and recommendations. However, we should do something else before we sail into action: extend a loving presence by listening. Listening is a solid prerequisite for action. If we immediately launch into explaining techniques, resources or goals it may distance or patronize the person we wish to help. It takes more vulnerability to be in the dark with someone who is in the dark, than it does to stand outside and talk about the light. To say, "I do not understand, could you help me help you," unites two people in the bond of their fragility. Being with someone, sharing their pain and listening with the heart creates a caring climate. A true sincerity of motive finds its roots in love, forgetfulness of self and the desire to encourage, assist and enable. One must be *with* the other before doing *for* the other. Therapeutic actions may not be the most important priority. These actions may even shield us from the powerlessness we find in doing nothing. A quiet time to be receptive and present, with no more than a hand to hold, may seem so little yet be so much. A healing presence may bring forth in the one who suffers the inner resources to evoke a will to live that sees beyond the limitations of the present.

Healing can begin underneath the surface levels of financial difficulties, family troubles, or the stresses and fears of urban life.

A change of focus on our part can result in a clearer vision and a more positive, God-oriented perspective. The problems remain but we view them in a new light. Because healing can be a process of becoming whole, it is a lifelong integration of the many attributes and aspects of our lives. Integration only reaches perfection when we experience the beatific vision. If we think we are in a state of perfect integration, we may experience artificial security and become lazy, sloppy or reckless. Because pain has the ability to open the mind to great things, it can give us courage we never knew we had by showing us how God can bring good out of anything. Pain is only evil when we let it conquer us. When our body, mind or soul are wounded, we should remember all are in need of care.

It is our wounds that bring us to the desert most often. True, we feel alone and afraid. However, deep down in the solitude and silence of our hearts, at the place where wounds have not penetrated or scarred, we know God is more real and more present to us. It is there where we find that graces often have unpleasing wrappings.

> God is my great desire,
> His face I seek the first;
> To him my heart and soul aspire,
> For him I thirst.
> As one in desert lands,
> Whose very flesh is flame,
> In burning love I lift my hands
> And bless his name.
>
> God is my true delight,
> My richest feast his praise
> Through silent watches of the night,
> Through all my days.
> To him my spirit clings,
> On him my soul is cast;
> Beneath the shadow of his wings
> He holds me fast.

Timothy Dudley-Smith

A Serious Look at Sin

Sin divides and separates the body of Christ. Every evil in the world is present in each one of us. The more we sin, the more we open ourselves to the possibility of greater sin. Evil begets evil, and all external signs of sin in the world began from within us as quiet temptations which grew into sins through our choice.

We feel the insidious pull of temptation toward evil. Faith, grace, and the desire to do good aids us in not acting on these evil inclinations. Because sin pulls us away from God, it divides and alienates us from each other. Through sin we ignore, neglect or negatively respond to the needs of others. Sin weakens our friendship with God. Mortal sin destroys it. Sin focuses on self, yet even the smallest of sins has its effect on others. Sin mutters "I don't care" when there is a possibility to do something with care. Every sin has personal and social ramifications.

Once upon a time there were two teenage sisters. On a school morning one of them borrowed the other's new sweater without asking. They got into a terrible fight. Their father became upset, went to work, and berated his secretary. Because of this, she had a bad day, went home and shouted at her children. The mother of the girls went shopping. She was angry and could not find what she wanted. She snapped at the cashier. The cashier went home crabby. The teenage girls had a dreadful day at school. Nothing went right.

This example illustrates the social aspects of sin. Like the ripples flowing outward from a pebble thrown in a lake, so sin affects more people than the one who commits it. Sin divides and forgiveness reconciles. The more we reconcile with ourselves and others, the more we strengthen the body of Christ. The more we forgive, the more we connect with others. Frequent forgiveness brings us closer to Jesus. We try to bring him to others as we reach out with his love and touch others with his hope. Forgiveness breaks down hostility and indifference and diffuses them with generosity and the healing of reconciliation. Teresa keeps us pointed in the right direction: "Let us strive then always to look at the virtues and the good qualities which we find in others, and to keep our own grievous sins before our eyes."

At any moment, up to the moment of death, we can choose to separate ourselves from God. A beneficial way to remain in contact with the deserts of our own sins is through frequent examinations of conscience. When we practice this exercise, in an assiduous manner, it keeps us on the humble path with our eyes open and hearts trusting in God's mercy. Although we are aware of the stumbling stones of our sinful natures and inclinations, we walk ahead with faith and hope. Sometimes our humble path seems straight and well-defined. Other times it meanders, is lost in a shroud of fog or disappears in a trackless waste.

Appropriate self-examination is never easy. The fog that limits our inner vision can well blur our direction. To stray or detour from the humble path that leads us to God is very easy. Many roads can take us to the denial trail at the mere mention of sin. Our habitual, significant sins are downsized to small faults or foibles. We procrastinate or make excuses for not receiving the Sacrament of Reconciliation. If we become pedantic, plodding or placid in moving forward on the spiritual journey, we are more prone to be sidetracked. Complacency and mediocrity are false oases that pamper our ego. Determination and perseverance keep us on the humble road even when, most of the time, all signs of progress are gone and we find the same old sins, failures and weaknesses.

Perseverance and a few guidelines help us keep going on this difficult path. Self-examination should not bog us down or fill us with undue remorse. The four R's essential for an examination of conscience are: Reflection, Review, Repentance and Refocus. A few moments at the end of each day is a good time to look back over our day. We bypass routine and superfluous activities and concentrate on the feelings and longings of our heart. These findings can then be placed at the feet of Jesus by asking him to renew our faith in his love and mercy. The more we trust in God, the more we trust in our own strengths as they are reinforced by grace. Grace also clarifies our inner vision so that we can see how damaging our sins are to the mystical body of Christ. The more we are aware of God's beauty in and through us, the deeper our contrition will be.

If we look at ourselves but can only find negatives, we are straying from the path of humility. A fruitful way of avoiding this wrong turn is a grateful reflection on God's particular gifts to us this day. By focusing on both our sins and God's gifts, during our short examination, our contrition and gratitude become more sincere. In this way, we acknowledge what we have done without scruples or depression, are sorry and ask for God's mercy. By resolving to try again, we give our lives to God, trusting him to help us over and over again. The Sacrament of Reconciliation, as a mighty fortress, is always there to help us and give us strength to face our temptations and sins. One of the transforming beauties of the desert is a greater respect for, and deeper appreciation of, the awesome mysteries within each sacrament of the Church.

In moments of the desert's blinding light we see sin as it really is: the misuse of our free will. Every decision we make is either for God's glory or for our own. We were created with free will so we can love God freely. How often we do err in this. Because human weakness is the culprit in sin, we cannot blame God for the evils in the world. They come from ourselves, because we make poor decisions of judgment, will or purpose. Who are the hot-headed, haughty individuals who think they know it all? Who is careless, indifferent, rebellious and brash? We need only go to a mirror for the answer. The errors of our ways cause separation and sorrow. Separation and sorrow are the consequence of sin and no two sorrows from it are the same. However, God brings good out of the evil ways of humanity. With his strength we focus on the problems instead of the blame. We become emotionally stable enough to resist temptations and keep our negative impulses in check. Yes, we know that evil proliferates itself but, with a stronger force, so does good.

If we are over-critical or, conversely, too self-congratulatory, we can get bogged down on the path of humility. To reflect only upon the flaws in our characters, relationships or work by disregarding the sincere praise of others, or vice versa, creates an imbalanced orientation. Many things we do produce positive and negative results. A realistic self-appraisal helps us to avoid being too quick to blame or praise ourselves when things go wrong or right. Accuracy in examination of conscience occurs when we are neither too hard nor too soft on ourselves or others, nor overly critical or unrealistically positive. People who are motivated by doubts and expected failures learn little in life. Discouragement comes easily to poor souls who slosh around in pessimism and negativism in the swamp of disasters. Their woe-is-me outlook can be a slide down into learned helplessness or perennial victimhood. Swept backwards by the winds of fear and remorse they may recline, corpse-like, and await the inevitable. Such wearisome wretches are unable to use an examination of conscience in an appropriate way.

Conversion requires new thoughts, actions and behaviors that arise from a gospel-oriented outlook on life. Each effort toward conversion charges the spiritual batteries that facilitate moving ahead. As we move we refine feelings and values in our desire to stop destructive behaviors. Spiritual and emotional preparation must accompany a change in a particular behavior. If the change in behavior happens by itself that act may generate conflict or a predisposed sense of failure in other areas. Frequently change involves serious prayer, realistic desires, orderly plans and appropriate actions. Usually change is not simple, quick or the result of some desired fantasy. Conversely, on some occasions we can wait forever and never feel ready. We may be indecisive because our known concerns are more comfortable than unknown ones that come about through change. On rare occasions we move quickly and spontaneously, and trust in God beyond measure. Common patterns of change are made up of stepping stones that give us some short term satisfaction, eventually leading us on to the desired result. The first step begins with prayer and thought. Subsequent steps find creativity and an openness to new ideas and designs. Realistic external actions follow common sense thoughts and significant prayer. The bud of a desired virtue needs attention, nourishment and tenderness within, before it can blossom forth in beauty for others. When they come from strong roots, virtuous actions are consistent and become refined through practice.

True virtue progresses to practical application. False virtue regresses to its relational vice. A virtue is a good habit that enables an individual to act rightly in accord with enlightenments of faith. The root virtue in the examination environment is forgiveness. The more we forgive ourselves the greater our compassion will be toward the shortcomings of others. Frequent forgiveness of ourselves and others will keep us honest and flexible. Forgiveness is the most beautiful expression of love. Each time we authentically forgive, we let go of negatives, release grievances, recriminations and blame. We receive peace of mind and healing of soul. Forgiveness goes beyond a feeling, emotion or sentiment. It is more of a decision. An action follows regarding what has been decided. The action reaches beyond glossing over things that hurt us to a concrete choice to deal with our hurt in a constructive way. Such decisions help us move forward unfettered by the baggage of negative attitudes. We have the potential for good and for evil and are capable of corresponding acts. We also know it is better to forgive rather than to nurse negative feelings that may lead to evil acts. Letting go of stored up or current negative thoughts clears the mind, improves our personal and social relationships, brightens our outlook and, of course, brings us nearer to God.

A Carmelite novice asked his director: "Why is everyone here so happy except me?" "They have learned to see goodness and beauty everywhere," the director said. "And why cannot I see goodness and beauty everywhere?" asked the novice. "Because you cannot find outside what you fail to see within yourself," came the reply from the director. If we focus on goodness and beauty within us, we will find them easier to discover in others. Wisdom guides us in our feelings, thoughts, and in the responsible actions that result from them. We learn to react moderately with emotional responses that are warm or cool. Such responses allows for God's beauty to filter through our feelings.

A hot emotional response may block beauty by strong but inaccurately preconceived ideas. It is easy to push others away because they are different from us. Prejudice bolsters the "we are number one" nonsense. If we were number one, others would be number two, three and so on. This superior attitude distorts the body of Christ and is responsible for stereotypes, injustice, greed, violence and wars. Cold emotional responses may be the result of a lackluster life, or a high sense of self-satisfaction. They are apt to occlude the passages within the heart, or shrivel the heart.

Hot or cold emotional responses may invoke arguments within a group of which we are a part. Leaving the group would cause more disorder. In such a case mental withdrawal into being with Christ and saying silently to him: "I know you are here" may calm the atmosphere. This quiet act of faith leads us to discover we can say something quite sensible in the tensest of situations.

God is love and through God and his love for us we learn. In order to experience goodness at our inmost center, we must be good as we outwardly express the goodness of Jesus to others in quiet ways. Teresa goes to the heart of love for us: "Love consists not in the extent of our happiness, but in the firmness of our determination to try and please God in everything, and to endeavor, in all possible ways, not to offend him." In our struggle for sanctity, the Sacrament of Reconciliation offers channels of efficacious graces which unify and strengthen us, individually, so that we resist temptation, and collectively, in the mystical body of Christ.

God is like a painter painting our portrait. We pray, make sacrifices, try to live according to his love and wonder what he is dabbing on his canvas. We reach the limits of our endurance and want to see what we look like through God's eyes. God smiles at us and says, "You'll see your portrait when it is finished. If you see it now, you are not going to like it. It's a caricature at most, but in itself it is nothing to look at for now. Wait and see. In due time, I will finish the work and it will be shown." We may look at our portrait, but will only see its unique beauty when God is finished with it. We may not like or understand it at present. Some stray lines or a few haphazard colors will not make sense. At times, many of us feel that life does not make sense. God cautions us to wait a little while and have patience. The portrait is incomplete, but the result will justify the long wait. Then we will sincerely appreciate the work and gratefully thank the painter.

In the desert Carmelites experience life at its heights and depths. Much is asked and much is given. Although it is fraught with unknowns, the desert entices the Carmelite with its haunting, clarion call. Carmel becomes a way of life and a growth in life. The great gifts and trials of the desert keep the Carmelite directed toward God. The arid space and empty time places a hectic pace and packed days in the background. The stark quiet of desert experiences punctures modern environments. It becomes known that pilgrims in Carmel can live in a rushed and busy world without becoming a part of it.

As with an artist's painting, the spiritual journey takes place one step at a time. Prayer can be unappetizing, yet nourishing and sustaining. Without prayer Carmelites would quickly die in the desert heat. With a burning seal the desert confirms that a

Carmelite is, first and foremost, before anything else, a person of prayer. Although Carmelites may be identified by other titles, our most important identity is one who is faithful to prayer. Prayer is as necessary to our life as a beating heart.

A Carmelite lives the prayer of Christ. Authentic Carmelite prayer is not seen by others. It is lived alone and in quiet, as did Jesus when he went into the desert to pray. Christ is found mainly in solitude and is given to others in unnoticed ways. The more we give Jesus to others in unobtrusive ways, the more real our prayer of the desert becomes. There are no specific deeds or words or ministries. Jesus is passed on to others in ways unmeasured, unnoticed and as unseen as the clear, still desert air.

Sensitive people see Jesus within the Carmelite without the Carmelite doing or saying anything. Jesus is lived from the depths of the soul where there are empty hands and no words. Carmel is a mystery and a walk in the twilight or dark night. Often the walk is lonely, but by being alone we learn the deeper values of love. Love takes on numerous forms, many of which are hard to recognize. Deep mysteries and mystical oases are part of the desert. Carmelites live in mystery. Most of the time the effects of desert prayer remain unknown. Mystery reveals strange changes. What were thought of as unbearable trials become vessels of blessings. Dark nights in the desert leave an emptiness and a void which makes no sense. They are more about letting go than moving ahead. When the light returns there is more strength because of the dark. Carmelites find benedictions in crosses which are both humbling and exhilarating. As we empty ourselves of our own realities, we experience the wonder and beauty of God working in and through our uniqueness in his reality.

A Carmelite strives to live the prayer of Jesus in the barren desert. With each step an inner voice repeats the words of John Donne: "Take me to you. Imprison me. For I, except you enthrall me, never shall be free, or ever chaste, except you ravish me."

The Challenge and the Gift

We are all flawed in one way or another. Defects are found in our bodies, in our temperaments, and in our souls. Our psychological, social and cognitive processes are other areas that can be affected. God made us as fragile and vulnerable human beings. Perhaps he did so to make us more caring toward each other.

Each of us is precious to God and in need of others. As we realize this we strive to respect the diversity and variation in our abilities and disabilities. We broaden our perception of disability when we find it can lead to new abilities. A specific ability may lead to a disability when it becomes so time-consuming it blocks development in other areas in our lives.

Respect for the uniqueness of each human life is a small current in the mainstream of secular society. The mainstream forcefully flows with ultra-selfishness and independence, and passing in fear of those who are not physically attractive or mentally strong. It is of vital importance that the small current become wider. The more the concepts of secular society grow, the less we become a community. The handicaps of the young, the vulnerabilities of middle age and the infirmities of the old contain positive forces that can bring unity in diversity.

Sharing our frailties can replace self-pity and undue dependence on others. The processes of life are both enabling and disabling. Most of us will face the eventual reality of physiological deterioration as we grow old. Only our souls are made to last forever. Our fragile vessels will decay in the earth and our souls will, if we have lived well, travel on to new life with the resurrected Christ.

Small elements of Jesus' resurrection can be found in the technologies of rehabilitation. Those who successfully experience rehabilitation programs experience traces of new life. We are reborn as we overcome struggle, survive, and thrive. Each step past the confines of impairment is a confirmation of the value of life and the strength of the human spirit.

We need to hold hands, not in mutual pity or saccharine sentiment, but in a renewal of the recognition of the gift and dignity of life. People with terminal illnesses might think they want to die, but what lies below that thought? Perhaps they want to know if they are still loved, still special or still worthwhile. Perhaps they want to know they will not be abandoned or seen as a burden. Perhaps they want reassurance that they will grow in and through the illness. Perhaps it is a plea that they will be cared for even though they are not the same as they were before. Those who verbalize a plea to die may not be able to verbalize a cry to live.

Fragments of Easter are seen in those who lose an ability, but learn positive ways to work around the loss. Life takes small, and sometimes large, chunks from our physical and mental capacities. As we err when we judge a book by its cover, so do we err when we judge a person by his or her color, shape, physical or mental characteristics. We pass through our cultural definitions of physical or mental perfection when we realize those with physiological flaws may have luminous, thriving souls. Conversely, those who are physically beautiful or mentally advanced may have souls that are dismal or decrepit.

Disabilities may be a unifying link in our need for each other and our dependence on God. The threads of life are rich in colors and weave together more strongly when we help each other with authentic needs and live the gospel message. Verbal expression of a modest need can be the beginning of a serious conversation. A small request may help another feel needed. Blunt reality says our perceived independence separates, alienates and segregates us one from another. Excessive independence weakens our community and Church. We need to recognize and practice our basic interdependence, rooted as it is in the love of Christ which bonds us together for the good of each other.

The way we individually interpret our suffering signifies our uniqueness. No other person will completely understand how our pain affects us physically, emotionally or spiritually. Each aspect is affected and all interrelate with a positive or negative influence on ourselves and others. A man who suddenly loses his sight will, no doubt, experience anger, confusion or depression. He may blame God for his loss and lash out at his loved ones. Much later, with the aid of graces, there is a change in his strong negative reactions. They transform into perseverance, courage and hope. He becomes an inspiration to others. Indeed, our reactions to suffering can break us or make us.

Love directs us to deal with our suffering in a positive way. We enter the pain and live with it with realistic expectation and respect. We trust God in our suffering, knowing it can be a channel for personal and spiritual growth. We fluctuate within the limits of our endurance, neither by being stoic and placing ourselves above the pain, nor by being consumed and becoming a product of the pain.

Everything in life happens for a purpose. Although we may not understand the total purpose in suffering, we can find specific areas that enlighten us with new wisdom. Finding meaning in our pain comes from a combination of effort and grace. Moving through pain with assisting graces brings us out of dark tunnels into the light of possibilities. We find pieces that answer the puzzling question: "What can I make from the situation in which I am?"

A mother's only child dies. A couple, whose child died a few years ago, spends quiet time with her at the funeral home and after the burial. Their silent presence does more for the mother than most of the words well-meaning people offer. Silent presence is a start in the long process of healing.

The greater we love the greater our potential is for positive suffering. Coping with a small pain in a positive way helps us cope with bigger pains in different circumstances. Pain can purge false pride, conceit or any other attitude that masks our true selves. As our renewed personalities bloom forth, we become more thoughtful and sensitive. Knowing God better is more important to us than trying to find answers. Many people would not find deeper meaning in their lives nor real faith in God without problems to overcome. God's graces help us cultivate and cope with things we cannot change. Our earthly life is a passage and after a few painful struggles we can find a deeper peace and greater love. Growing in love is the greatest adventure in our lives. It asks for great risks, openness without reserve, facing others without pretense and waiting for answers that may not come. Pain and love make us vulnerable. C.S. Lewis wrote: "Love anything and your heart will certainly be wrung and possibly broken. If you want to make sure of keeping it intact, you must give your heart to no one, not even an animal. Wrap it carefully round with hobbies and little luxuries; avoid all entanglements, lock it up safe in the casket or coffin of your selfishness. But in that casket — safe, dark, motionless, airless — it will change. It will not be broken; it will become unbreakable, impenetrable, irredeemable."

If we risk to love, we love ourselves in such a way that allows us to be deeply loved by God. Love helps us to pray and work. It unites us to God and to each other. Love takes us from personal prayer to practical service. The people and events in the world then bring us back to prayer. If we love others we desire for them far more than what is in our power to give them. This is what leads us back to prayer.

Love's genesis begins in God and moves to the heart of the soul. A sound awareness of this imparts a vision that opens the heart to embrace that which it does not understand. Our actions and expressions flow from our love. The source of our love is the divine love of God that dwells in us. Sometimes our love flows wide and free, but at other times trickles, narrowly and restrictively. The changes in flow come from our current awareness of God and his work within us. The amounts of love we give, like the sources for our motivation, can change so often.

The more we give love the more fertile our souls become to

God's love and the love others bear for us. It is beautiful to realize God's love through the love and care shown to us by others. Through this gift, we will find that we wish to love more than we wish to receive love. The love that takes us to the door of a friend, or the heart of a stranger, may be the voice of God within us urging us toward something very profound.

The struggles involved in trust and sacrifice are essential parts of love between friends and families. Parents who cling to their adult children, adult children who are overly dependent on their parents, and friends who use each other do not express this type of love. True sacrifice leaves the other to come and go, speak or remain silent, comfort or confront. Love grows if it is fed and watered, weeded and pruned. It requires work and effort. Love asks more than what seems possible and stretches us beyond the limits of vision we set for ourselves. Those who truly love provoke us to a greater goodness by keeping us uncomfortable with mediocrity. True lovers are great treasures, but the ones they love will never know them completely. Each person has elements of mystery and is really known only by God.

In the fifteenth century, in a tiny village near Nuremberg, there lived a family, with eighteen children. In order to feed his family the father, a goldsmith, worked almost eighteen hours a day at his trade and at any other kind of job he could find. Despite their seemingly hopeless condition, two of the children had a dream. They both wanted to pursue the study of art. However, they knew their father would not be financially able to send either of them to Nuremberg to study at the academy.

After long discussions the two boys worked out a pact. They would toss a coin. The loser would work in the nearby mines and his earnings would support his brother who would attend the academy. Then, when that brother finished his studies, he would support the other brother as he attended the academy. They tossed a coin after church one Sunday. Albrecht Dürer won the toss and went off to Nuremberg. Albert went to the mines and worked in them for four years. As was promised, he financed his brother, whose work at the academy was quite a sensation. Albrecht's etchings, woodcuts and oils were better than those of many of his professors.

When the young artist returned to his village the Dürer family held a festive dinner to celebrate. After a memorable meal, Albrecht rose from his place of honor and made a toast to his beloved brother. His closing words were, "And now, Albert, blessed brother of mine, now it is your turn. You can go to Nuremberg to pursue your dream and I will take care of you." Albert shook his lowered head. He said no, he could not go to Nuremberg. It was too late. Four years in the mines destroyed his hands. The bones in his fingers were often broken because of his work. His hands were stiff and sore. The arthritis was so bad in his right hand that he could not hold a glass to return the toast. To draw delicate lines on canvas would be impossible.

More than 450 years have passed. Albrecht Dürer's masterful portraits, woodcuts, sketches and other works are in great museums all over the world. However, most people are probably familiar with only one of his works. One day, to pay homage to Albert for all he had sacrificed, Albrecht painstakingly drew his brother's abused hands with palms together and fingers skyward. He called this masterpiece "Hands." We know this tribute of love as "The Praying Hands."

5

Traveling Light

'Tis a gift to be simple, 'tis a gift to be free. 'Tis a gift to come down where we ought to be. And when we come down to the place just right, it will be in the valley of love and delight. When that true simplicity is gained, to bow and to bend we shan't be ashamed. Turn, turn, 'twill be our delight. 'Til by turning and turning we come 'round right.   *Quaker Hymn*

The gifts in this lovely song permeate us with lightsome beauty. They guide us toward relaxation in the peace and presence of God who is within and around us. By turning and turning to God we meet reality in its simplest and most direct form. Our turning takes courage, for the more we turn the less we have on which to hold. However, as our trust in divine providence grows, we find that less is more.

There seems to be a particularly clever way of catching monkeys in India. The story is told that hunters cut a hole in a coconut which is just large enough for the monkey to put in his paw. Then two smaller holes are drilled at the other end, through which a wire is passed. The coconut is secured to the base of a tree. The hunters put a banana inside the coconut and hide. The monkey finds the coconut, puts his paw inside and takes hold of the banana. As long as the monkey holds onto the banana he cannot get his paw out. In order to free himself all the monkey has to do is let go of the banana. It seems that most monkeys do not let go.

Our minds can get caught in the very same way. Cultivating the habit of letting go is fundamental to a lighter and simpler journey in life. As we pay attention to our inner journey, we rapidly discover certain thoughts, feelings and situations which we may dwell on beyond the point of practicality or common sense, stretching them into fantasy. Similarly we may spend too much time trying to rid or protect ourselves from thoughts, feelings or situations that are unpleasant or painful. Indeed, negative memories can be very disturbing or frightening. Individuals who hold onto these memories may be people who are actually happy being unhappy or who are fascinated with the grim. How we choose to interpret our thoughts can determine if we are victims or creators. Our memories can keep us paddling in our little pool of self-pity, or help us swim in the river of life. Do we grumble about our situation, or implement new ideas to improve it?

If we are overly concerned about our past experiences, we need to put aside the tendency to prolong the memories that elevate or depress us. By doing so, we eventually let them go. We let things be as they are and accept them as best as we are able. After we realize our minds are grasping at or pushing away certain thoughts, we can more readily stop these actions. If something has a strong hold in our minds for a long period of time, and we find it difficult to let go of it, we might direct our attention to what our hold on it represents or why we hold it. An inordinate hold defines our attachments and prevents clear thinking. If we relax our grasp, the consequences of our attachments may be revealed to us as well as how it might feel if we let go of them completely.

Feelings are part and parcel of change. They show up even when we do not expect them and are normal in any transition. A simple change in diet may cause us to feel envy toward those who can eat what we cannot, or feel frustration at the reason for the diet. Joy, happiness and laughter often come into our lives when they are not anticipated or expected. Happiness rarely comes if it is pursued, like the pot of gold at the end of a rainbow. Often it happens as surprises along the way. Sadness can dim the most joyous occasion in an instant. As the sunlight pierces through dark clouds, so can laughter brighten a painful time. Joy comes to us as we rise above ourselves by an ascent of the heart and give of ourselves for the good of others. Efforts to pursue, capture or hold on to things that gave us happiness or sadness in the past rarely keep us happy or sad in the present. Grace and time change us as we move ahead in faith.

Looking at the ways in which we hold on to things we do not need, ultimately shows us something about the experience of the opposite action. Letting go is not as difficult as we might imagine. We do it every night when we go to sleep. Yes, it is good to remember our past. It has much to tell and teach us. Our pleasant memories are like votive candles burning at the sacred places in our hearts. It is also good to look at our future. Our hopes and dreams give meaning and depth to the present. However, neither past memories or future imaginings should rob us of the living life at the present. The present moment is a gift received only to the extent of our presence in it.

To detach ourselves from self-serving attitudes is a lifelong task. Sweets from Job's comforters nurse our hurt feelings of pride, resentment, anger and pain. Oh how free we would be if we let these attitudes go. However, the comforters' confections are sticky as they give superficial solace to our bruised egos. Pity parties may be sweet help for the moment, but offer no lasting nourishment. Knee-jerk reactions and decisions are common and frequently based on impulse or the emotion of the moment. Common sense and prudence tell us more time is required for our thinking selves to make sound decisions. When we can separate our feeling selves from our thinking selves, we place attention on the latter and then observe how our self-serving attitudes diminish our freedom. We can grieve and cry over our past hurts, then let them go instead of hanging on to them for dear life. Those in victimhood blame others and make themselves out to be the best of the worst. Who needs the cumbersome baggage of self-serving attitudes on the spiritual journey? If we really open our eyes, we can look deep into our problems or hurts and discover liberating opportunities in them. Indeed, we can give in to our conditions or stand up to them and then move on.

When we let go of false sources of security, we are better able to understand what it means to trust in God. Walls are easily built to protect ourselves from hurt, disappointments and failures. Yet, they keep out sunlight, fresh air and rain that help our seedlings of life to grow. Too much protection causes seedlings to remain as seedlings. How easy it is to build thick protective walls. Like an over-abundance of insurance policies, they can provide security from most kinds of danger and even keep out God himself. A sound trust in God is the real source of security. Better spiritual health can come about through appropriate use of our sorrows, tribulations or failures. Each may represent a certain dying followed by new life. Dying is never absent from life. Its varied dimensions are frequently present in our living. Dying comes through experiences that diminish or grate against us. However, all forms of dying can open us up to receive, reform and grow toward God by discovering positive good in ourselves and others. As we die to self and the false securities of life, we rise to life in faith with God as our true protector.

Simple faith helps us accept responsibilities even though we do not feel completely trained or suited for them. Perhaps the person who gives us a responsibility sees something positive about us that we do not see. Being overly concerned about competence might lead to a rigid perfectionism. No one is perfect in anything all of the time. A relaxed grasp on what we do assists us in not being overly preoccupied by our jobs or responsibilities. After we free ourselves of the possessive entanglements of our careers, financial strategies, home securities or material goods, we can maintain a clearer focus on the benevolence of God. We know we can never insulate ourselves against misfortunes. However, under the surface of misfortunes, we sense that all will be well because

God is working in and through them.

Many so-called luxuries and comforts are not only dispensable but are also a hindrance to mental and spiritual growth. Luxuries, like children's toys, are a lot more fun if there are not too many of them. We need little to enjoy a happy life. To verify this, watch a child happily playing with the cardboard box in which all the toys that now surround him were stored. Despite this, in blatant and subliminal ways, consumerism lurks around many corners. It is true that a few comforts are nice, but too many of them lead to increases in time and money. An ability to distinguish need from want must remain intact during our battles with consumerism. The quality and quantity of the things we own and use, what we throw away, and how our expenses affect our lives tell much about what we value.

We can crowd our minds with memories, feelings, attitudes, musings about our gains or losses or the various luxuries in our lives. Such a firmly packed mind would find it difficult to meet a current challenge. This may also hold true for people who have more projects, meetings or errands than they can handle. Our minds need space and suppleness to create, probe or invent. A cluttered mind rarely maintains the flexibility needed to be attentive to new or small things. The extra effort, a few words of praise or thanks or the ability to spontaneously give the best we have comes from cognitive processes that are not on overload. An individual with a sharp, clear mind does not cut corners or produce slipshod results, because new or little things handled carelessly lead to big problems. Clear, sound thinking keeps the mind tranquil and mobilizes it within the concerns of the present.

While a disagreeable incident may cause us to fuss and fret a little, with time and discipline our minds can return to the calm and rational expression of our thoughts. Long-term self-hate or self-glorification, and pessimistic or pollyannaish reflections on situations or problems about which we can do nothing, muddle and clog the mind. A viable mind is flexible and accurate. It is able to judge current teachings, movements and actions in the light of Christian truth. The ability to view current problems, inside and outside the Church, within the traditional teachings of Christian doctrine signifies mature thinking. Faith keeps what is necessary and lets go of the litter that we find in current theologies, Church fads or fashionable liturgical trends.

We can increase mind space for new challenges in several ways. If the things we do are not authentic needs, we give them up. We respect our limits and rarely go beyond their boundaries. We pass on to others errands and responsibilities that tax our energies beyond our limits. However, giving to another for the sake of the other is distinctly different from giving to another to increase our self-importance. We enhance the latter when we make many complaints about the vast amounts of work we must do, or the great number of phone calls or appointments we must make or keep. Such complaints make the coat worn by the false ego very thick and cumbersome. The warm sun of simple faith slowly decreases a need for that coat. Our self-importance diminishes when we can empty us of us. When we reach the point where we take off the coat for good, God can be God in us.

If we are without something we really need, the Lord provides in ways we never expected. If we launch into a new project, resources may appear before we need to ask for them. Within a simple faith mode the desire to bully, dominate or control is rare. Personal maturity places people above tasks or things. The gift of friendship means more than gifts of material goods. Quality time with others exceeds attending numerous meetings or exotic events. If we limit our obligations, we can maintain each obligation with integrity. All that is actually necessary is to meet our basic necessities and, if possible, sensible securities and enjoy a few comforts in life.

A simple life finds beauty in the commonplace. It maintains a respect for the world and its treasures. The beauty of being fruitful in what we do neutralizes an inordinate determination to achieve and excel. Fruit blossoms from the seeds of a genuine sense of responsibility. Most of the time, we complete our tasks with even composure and tranquility, instead of in haste or indolence. The discipline of inner quiet gives us the grace to appreciate life more and to slow down and be still for prayer and contemplation. An unhurried demeanor offers others the freedom to slow down and listen in. As we travel a little slower and listen a little longer we find snippets of Christian wisdom and practical insights in very interesting places.

Our fruitfulness flowers through the talents which God has bestowed on us. Doing something easily that others find difficult is a talent. Easily does not mean perfectly. The woods would be silent if no birds sang except the very best. How sad for those who never sing. They die with so much music inside them. We need to use the talents we possess even if they are not the best. Rare is the best there is, which we usually call genius. Practical talent shows itself in days that show balance. The tendency to schedule our days beyond our energies is impractical and self-destructive. Even if this schedule provides the pleasant feeling of being indispensable, it is still impractical. Who is indispensable? Now and then we like to fantasize we are, but harsh reality tells us we can be replaced, or entirely removed from the scene. Instead, let us allow room for some sweet mysteries in our daily routine. Then we shall be contentedly busy and constructively fruitful as we move ahead.

A Plain and Simple Walk

A walk with simplicity permits us to savor each step and to discover the dignity of each creature we meet. Our observations develop a respect for all people and all creation. We digress from this path if we live a lifestyle that exploits nature for excess profit or any other reason. We do not come to know the world by that which we take from it, but by that which we bring to it.

Our words create a good part of our world. Our use of language is a great part of our reality. Things are not good or bad of themselves. We label them as beautiful or ugly, expensive or cheap, fashionable or out of date. Resisting the urge to label or stereotype is a challenge. We might examine how, of what and to whom we speak. We need not have concern about what we say if we speak as truthfully as we can and understand the value of not speaking at certain times. If we say yes when we mean yes and no when we mean no, mixed signals can be brought to a minimum. Playing games in conversations congests our communication with others. Because we may assume that we know someone after living with or knowing him or her for years, we often anticipate what that person will say, feel or do, thus stunting the growth and mystery of being human. All things that "go without saying" between two people can build a mountain of miscommunication. We dare not assume anything about those with whom we live or work. We appreciate and savor the realization that human beings are complex and ever-changing, even if on the surface they appear to be unchanging. If we do not anticipate a person's words or actions, surprises will come to reveal new dimensions and new depths in an individual we thought we knew so well. When life descends to dull routine, we might imagine we are just meeting those with whom we live. We start by listening to their voices as if we are hearing them for the first time. As we attentively listen to the words, we may find new meaning in them. Problems, which may be part of our relationship with others, can now be viewed as friends or teachers. Problems can teach us patience, courage and creativity. When we speak and listen well, we are courteous, pleasant and kind. We avoid generalizations, categories, labels, strong opinions and bold declarations. We surrender our views if actions from them are harmful, destructive, or close off dialogue with others. We travel easier with less verbal baggage. We talk with gratitude for life in the mystery of the moment, then let it go. We quietly direct our thinking to redeeming qualities rather than ruminating about flaws. Simple expressions of gratitude have a soothing effect on those who receive them. As we speak gently we become more gentle with ourselves and others.

The ancient Sufis used to say: "Speak only after your words have passed through three doorways. At the first doorway ask: 'Are my words true?' If they are, let them pass. At the second doorway ask: 'Are my words necessary?' If they are, let them pass. At the third doorway ask: 'Are my words kind?' Only then let them pass the third gateway."

What we say, do, own, use, eat, wear, drive, and live in express much about who we are and tell us much about ourselves. What we desire we pursue. The way we get, take care of or give away things expresses our attitudes toward ourselves, others and God. What does idolatry mean? It is an immoderate attachment to something. We treat what we idolize as an absolute and we may have many absolutes in our lives. What gives us a sense of ourselves, absorbs our interests and gives us meaning? Many identify themselves and their security with what they say, do, own, use, eat, wear, drive, or live in.

A tourist from a distant country went to visit a famous rabbi. The tourist was amazed that the rabbi's home was a bare room with a bed, table, bench and a few books. "Where is your furniture?" asked the tourist. "Where is yours?" asked the rabbi. "Furniture? I am just passing through" replied the tourist. "So am I" said the rabbi.

Detachment demands sacrifice. We leave behind that which prevents us from going to God. Detachment from possessions, money and status symbols are possible when there is no addiction to them. Immoderate attachments become addictive when life is not tolerable without them. Letting go, especially of things that give us unrestrained pleasure or things we thought we could never live without, is painful. This pain needs to be acknowledged. Detachment blesses us with glorious indifference to possessions or positions. We care, but are not inordinately attached to what we have or do. We show genuine interest in and are responsible for that which is entrusted to our care. We also can give it up if we feel a genuine call to have or do something else. Through detachment we have rare need for more and freedom from the strain to get ahead. We enjoy an interior tranquility, trusting in the gracious provisions of God. We gently accept periods of restlessness that come and go as part of life.

Detachment helps us not to hold on to dark grumbles or negative inclinations for long. If we are not as close to God as we once were, we make no mistake about who moved. If certain people have an irritating effect on us for any length of time, we strive to refrain from irrational confrontations or rough words. Rather than boiling or steaming about them, we try to send quiet, peaceable beams of prayer their way. It takes gumption to rise above our negative feelings, but this is a resolute move toward God. We can also direct our prayer beams to those whom we do not know, near or far, who are hurting or indifferent. Through our prayerful concern we link them with the light of Christ. Furthermore, our beams to others release concentration on the bruises of our egos as we quietly join these people with Jesus. This quiet bonding offers them the grace of God's presence even if they may not consciously be aware of it.

As Carmelites we strive to show others our appreciation for, and example of, a simple, ordinary life that is rooted in prayer. Thérèse of Lisieux, our beloved saint and doctor of the Church, advises us to be authentic through simplicity, detachment, humility and complete trust in the Lord. She lived these guiding lights on the road of Carmel exceptionally well. Through these lights we become more present to the world because we move deeper into the mysteries of God who is the source of unity for the world. Greater love, trust and hope are the fruits of faithful prayer. These fruits help all Christians stand firm in the midst of the storms of current movements that rage against gospel values. Through prayer and the other attributes of Carmel, we become more aware of what God is calling us to be and do.

The more we persevere in prayer, the easier it will be to let go of whatever keeps us away from God. Our personal reform must include grief and sorrow as we acknowledge our faults and sins. Indeed, forbidden fruit remains sweet to the taste. We know we are sinners in need of God's mercy and thank him for the Sacrament of Reconciliation. On our Carmelite journey, temptations to sin are always with us, like hounds, chasing and snapping at our heels. Temptations constantly invite escape into the ever-changing trends and hysteria of the world. Discipline of the senses seems remote during these times. There is so much in our world with which Christians can neither sympathize nor cooperate. However, we learn to stand on our own two feet with the discipline that strong soldiers of Christ require. Like Thérèse, we trust in God to work within us in times of temptation. Faithful and sometimes painful prayer changes us so that we no longer cling to that which is unnecessary in life.

Dying to the old self is painful. We find relief as we look beyond the pain to new life. Giving up fashionable positions, items we do not use, comfortable habits or lazy tendencies gives us the freedom to develop our untapped potential. Love, trust and hope help us to perceive what is happening and where it might lead us. We collect the facts and consider the consequences within the disciplines Jesus taught. These virtues are as lights eternal in all our darkness. They guide us in what we believe about ourselves and how we relate to those around us. Simple daily prayer keeps us from not moving beyond the ethical and moral boundaries of our Christian faith and gives clear witness to our Christian values. It does no good to sit up and take notice if we just keep on sitting. The love we try to give is challenging as it should be unfettered by expectations of repayment, reciprocation or rewards. Faith and hope support Christian love which is the foundation of a specific way of life. Christian love goes beyond the pressures of the moment, projections of a frightened ego, guilt, or fear in current chaos.

In a secular culture that often is cruel and opposes any witness to faith, we must attest to our Christian values. The measure of our faith is shown in what we do with the circumstances that surround our lives. Choices based on the teachings and knowledge of Jesus and his Church are not popular. However, it is said that the roots grow deep where the wind blows strong.

A Priceless Gift

Simplicity is a gift of liberation. It originates from within and is manifest in our external demeanor. We express simplicity to the degree in which we are aware of its internal reality. Love is the tap root of that reality. It unfolds in conduct that reflects an unassuming nature, authenticity and sincerity. An inner simplicity sees divine providence in all things and views most of life with a clear and fresh kind of beauty. We maintain beauty through love that has an honest and fair outlook and uses abilities unobtrusively. The more we love, the easier we forgive. The more we forgive, the lighter the luggage on our life's journey will be. Indeed, a destructive or negative mind set, however brief, dims the beauties in life.

Our journey to Jesus is easier with simplicity as a guideline. We can relax our grip on internal or external goods in ways we did not expect. We neither build up nor do we downgrade things that concern us nor dwell on our accomplishments or regrets. We are not overly concerned with success, health, making a good impression, the approval of others, spiritual status or the future. We find happiness and holiness in the call of the present. Our opportunity to love is that which keeps us from floundering in undue preoccupations with the past, present or future. We do what is needed, when it is needed even though we do not want to do it. Our awareness of God and his love increases in whatever comes along in our lives because we look beyond current perplexing situations and know somehow they will be a means for growth. We relax and experience relief because God oversees all and is present even if we cannot find him. Underneath the perplexities, tensions and weariness of life, we know that things are not as bleak or serious as we may think them to be.

The chances we take find roots of courage in the goodness of God. We find graces as we loosen up about life and take it easy. We discover and choose happiness in the imperfections of this world because we know who holds it together. We are happiest when we give of ourselves, and we are truly disturbed when anything in God's creation is exploited. Because faith is not based on sentiment or reason, it builds on trust and love and is steadfast, responsible, and committed. We wait for God in prayer at a place beyond our own sins and virtues. We wait and wait and at last find God in little, unexpected things. There is no longer a heavy dependence upon finding God in overtly holy events. Life becomes holy in its ordinariness. The location of our self-worth is in Christ, with no need for the highs or lows of ego. As we live our loyalty to God in the routine of our days, life itself is holy. Rare is our dependence on affirmation which comes from our favorite ministries, good friends or spiritual favors. We learn to love God for who he is, rather than for what he gives us. We freely share what we have with others, without thought for return. The more we experience liberation from internal and external stuff, the greater our realization of God will be. A lot of stuff can make dragons out of mites and can dull, stunt or sap our creativity, time or energy.

Simplicity looks at problems as more of a challenge than a curse. This view does not minimize, maximize, or deny what is there. A focus without clutter faces the problem squarely with an unblemished clarity. We rely on help from God, competent people and our own inner resources for solutions. As simplicity basks in the strength of self-discipline, we can direct our energies toward activities that change things for the better. Discipline recognizes the futility of endless debates, discussions and committee meetings that vaguely address the practical problems of life.

Most of us are moderately aware of the way simplicity works. It is a lifetime process of small movements. These movements open us to a greater receptivity to Jesus. Although we hardly notice our inner transformation, we know it has happened as we look back over the years. Indeed, our lives become more serene as our faith deepens.

Edith Stein was a convert, gifted teacher and writer, and Carmelite nun. Along with her sister Rosa, she was killed at Auschwitz. Edith gives us these words of counsel: "God is there in these moments of rest and can give us in a single instant exactly what we need. Then the rest of the day can take its course, under the same effort and strain perhaps, but in peace. And when night comes, and you look back over the day and see how fragmentary everything has been, and how much you planned that has gone undone, and all the reasons you have to be embarrassed and ashamed, just take everything exactly as it is, put it in God's hands and leave it with him. Then you will be able to rest in him — really rest — and start the next day as a new life."

The reality of Holy Saturday is a great teacher of simplicity. There is no suffering, death, resurrection or new life experiences. Theological insights, meaningful prayers and energizing religious activities are uncommon or utterly absent. We are washed out and kneel, empty, before God. God is now the vast unknown, the one whom we discover by chance. The way to him is not known. Slowly God finds us and fills our emptiness, drop by drop. We prostrate ourselves before him in our poverty, helplessness and nothingness. Holy Saturday simplicity is void of illuminations, mystical revelations or even dark nights. The path to the imageless, wordless God within us is mist-bound and prayer loses its savor and comfort. No method of meditation satisfies us. The more we move into plain prayer the less we say. The need for words departs as they become inadequate. In silence we realize our nothingness in the greatness of God. So taken are we by his magnificence, we rarely speak of our problems, needs or desires. We become available and remain faithful regardless of our ever-changing moods or feelings. We live our prayer and witness this deepest expression of who we are. Prayer keeps us spiritually awake and alive. It is our lifeline to eternity. We are no longer frightful of great gaps of silence in our prayer. God moves in the silence and we listen because silence fosters love and understanding far beyond what our minds and hearts can offer.

The simplicity of Holy Saturday appears as a plateau in our lives which helps us settle down in the stillness of God. Timeless moments where we lose ourselves in God are both fearsome and awesome. His presence is a source of spellbinding wonder. The unknowable and knowable God is omnipresent with absence of any composition or divisibility. The more we live in the presence of God, the more we become the persons we should be. Our Holy Saturday plateaus give us strength to be faithful to ordinary common prayer and work. Our prayer or work may be easy or difficult, rewarding or perplexing, calm or distracting. Most areas within these extremes will not affect our interior peace. We live for God, belong to him and pray and work because we love him and his people. The simplicity of Holy Saturday calls us to cling to God in stark faith when our prayer seems stagnant, our work meaningless and our path ahead unknown.

The challenge of simplicity is to live as unwritten gospels and to place the imprint of God's love on others. We attain this by our response to God and others. We turn from what we receive on our inner journey and give Jesus to others through active care and prayer. In our unique and never to be duplicated way, we seek to live Jesus as we help others to experience love and bring out the good in them. The infusion of God's love into society brings wisdom to scientific knowledge, reverence to technology and the sacred to routine daily tasks. God is firmly established as our central reference point. As we look out from this point, simplicity reveals how often God helps us live with paradox or in a climate of uncertainty. Life is never completely in order, but grace keeps our horizons in focus. We shed the weight of need for approval or control and dilute or eliminate the toxins that are in our thoughts, emotions, relationships or activities. The pristine beauty of our fidelity to commitments becomes more apparent after the bloom is off our entrusted roses. Interior harmony renews our sense of belonging to and being interdependent with humanity. As we see the good in people and the mystery that resides in their hearts, we see the love of God.

Simplicity gives us the freedom to be nothing so God can use us for anything. He stretches us to our limits and beyond as we move closer to him through things that efface and enrich us. Now we feel more at home with struggle than with pleasure, which is a mystery to us.

With the Heart of a Child

Simplicity comes full circle when we capture the vision of a child before selfishness. New beginnings are a delight. We renew our bond with God at the beginning of each day and give our hearts to him as innocent children. Each passing day is a fresh offering of ourselves to God so that he may use us as he pleases. As we make our daily oblation, we are not overly concerned about the disruptive events that may happen to us. With childlike trust, we believe God will carry us through life as a loving father carries his child.

A simple wonder leads us to easy fascination at work, play or prayer. A humorous or refreshing comment breaks the pressure of the moment. The serendipities of life greet us as cheery surprises. In stillness there is holiness. No day dawns the same as another, but each has magical, spontaneous movements, bringing light to dark places and lifting droopy spirits. To be spiritually childlike is to be neither naive nor a babbler of spiritual baby talk. We watch

God with a sacred focus and do not lose sight of him by making detours on the road to him. Often detours, however good, become an end in themselves or tangle us up in fad spirituality for a long time. The simplicity of the child sees God as friend, guide and goal, without whom nothing can be done or no one can move forward. A childlike heart finds unconstrained joy in quiet conversation, honest expression of affection, simple pleasures and playful fun. A carefree trust in divine providence places searches and doubts in God's hands. Our work becomes more creative, laughter more spontaneous and sorrows more piercing. Even though we frequently stumble, we likewise get up and try again with a light heart. Trying again comes easily as it bubbles with trust. We are free to be ourselves, getting up quickly to begin anew. We are forthright and transparent, which is so refreshing in a world of duplicity. Yes, we know God watches all things and is by our side with the support of a loving father.

The graces of a child are ours as we get caught up in spellbinding wonder at a blackberry patch or fireflies in a jar. We find delight beyond reason as we watch water dripping from an icicle or note the path of a fluttering butterfly. A spring rain or simple sparrow is beautiful in novel ways. Caring for a garden, looking at a rainbow, mending clothes or doing volunteer work adds new dimensions of satisfaction to a simply lived life. The changing light on a lake, copper pennies, card tricks, a silly riddle or waddling ducks become magical and hold alluring charm. Sand sculpture or a jigsaw puzzle, a swing or crayons, are opportunities for pure delight and new discoveries. As we rediscover childlike delights our demeanor is blessed by a keen unsophisticated joy. Prayer is simply loving God with a love that is more surely given and warmly received. We pray in silence with open and abiding trust. The beauty of God's Spirit is within us, so far beyond our understanding, yet so reassuring and comforting. Life becomes unsophisticated and holds new or renewed adventures. A tattered, patched teddy bear with a happy grin brings sun to a gloomy day. He is so irresistible that when we look at him intensely we cannot stay sad or mad for long. For the young at heart, teddy has many magical, lovable, qualities. Sometimes, simplicity helps us to see ourselves as God's teddy bears. He may hug us or put us in a corner and forget us. Whatever he does it would not matter. It is enough for us to be there and to love him.

With Thérèse of the Child Jesus as our companion, we can learn how simplicity takes us along her little way to God. Her way is simple but not easy. We study her life and teachings, and with her words in prose we say:

> I come before you
> with empty hands....
> all the secret store of grace
> I fling into needy hearts,
> crying in the bitter night
> of fear and loneliness....
> Spendthrift of your Love
> I keep before me
> your empty hands....
> empty and riven
> with the great nails
> hollowing out
> rivers of mercy....
> until all your substance
> was poured out....
> So, I, my Jesus,
> with hands emptied
> for your love
> stand confident
> before your Cross,
> love's crimson emblem.
> It is the empty
> who are filled:

those who have made
themselves spendthrifts
for you alone,
fill the least
of your brethren
while they themselves
are nourished by your Love....
more and more emptied
that they may be filled
with you.

Carmel of Terre Haute

6

Body and Soul

God's might to direct me, God's power to protect me,
God's wisdom for learning, God's eye for discerning,
God's ear for my hearing, God's word for my clearing.
Early Gaelic Hymn

Sophocles, the great Greek dramatist, stated that the human body was the most wondrous of the world's wonders. Several centuries of scientific discoveries reconfirm and elevate these words. The body human is far more wondrous than Sophocles ever imagined.

Our bodies are composed of perishable matter, with the exception of that which they house, our souls. God is present in the still, imageless essence of our souls; the most real part of us that lives forever. Body, mind and soul need food, care and attention for survival. The soul is the vital life force of the body and mind, and vessel of a living flame of love kindled by the divine torch of God's love. Those who neglect to nourish their souls are in a sorry state. The human person is composed of body and mind which are animated by the soul. Our souls lift our thoughts, hopes and aspirations to something higher than our physical or mental selves. The lights from soul power give us the strength to see the brightness of God in the dark places in our lives and in those of others. Our souls are splendorous continuations of ourselves that extend beyond time, space, dimension or mental constructs. The force that sustains and propels the soul's development is, of course, prayer.

Many elements in every area of development influence body,

mind and soul. Our physical well-being includes health, positive attitudes toward illnesses and injuries, nutrition, exercise, living environment and sensory and motor skills. Our psycho-social well-being includes our moods, emotional support systems, ability to express and be receptive to positive attributes, control of destructive tendencies, self-esteem, acceptance and expression of feelings, dealing with stress, and social relationships. Our intellectual well-being includes educational endeavors, work-related study, leisure, personal interests and hobbies, projects, current events and stimulating discussions. Our spiritual well-being includes prayer, worship, reverence, meditation, religious study, works of service, sacramental life, grace and faith. It is of worth to state here that we may be advanced in physical fitness, intellectual pursuits, or psycho-social acumen yet remain spiritually immature at any point in our lives.

It is interesting to note that every stride forward on the spiritual journey has its corresponding dangers. Every step we take that brings us higher up the spiritual mountain increases the depths of the valley into which we may fall. As we gaze into the valley, it is good to remember that if we believe ourselves to be notably advanced in the spiritual life, and enjoy superb relations with the most elegant and elevated of celestial beings, it is time to start the climb anew.

Assessment of our body, mind and soul must continue throughout our lives. There are always new ways in which we can direct ourselves toward the positive and good. To move toward an integration in which body, mind and soul easily interrelate is very important. A dominant intellect, strong emotions that are easy to activate, excessive concentration on the body, or a rigid mind set hinders explorations of the soul. Enrichment of the soul's development is a sensitive and complex process. By trying to act on love of truth, and disregarding the negative influence of this age, we can make many decisions every day that individually and collectively add up to show what kind of Christian people we are.

Everything we do reverberates throughout humanity in varying positive or negative ways. There are hundreds of ways in which we can choose to do good. Linked with prayer, these choices are calls from the heart of our souls, that echo God's love through society. We give expression to these inner promptings by doing the most good that is possible in our circumstances. The habits of our souls are nourished by the thoughts we think, words we say and things we do. Love is a habit of the soul if it is consistent in our lives rather than isolated in a few good deeds. While we may do great good works, this is not necessarily a sign of a conscience that has its orientation in God. Daily banal tasks and seemingly insignificant kindnesses done with love are indications of a viable soul. We need not go to inner city slums or foreign countries to find people who are in need. They usually await us in our families or immediate neighborhoods.

The quality which separates us most from God's other creatures is that we are made in his image. We are coupled with God in some refractive way which defies understanding. We are not the light or the source of the light. We are a reflection of the light of God as it shines on a mirror. Each of us is a unique fragment of a mirror that shines the lights of God's truth, understanding, knowledge and love. Our personal reflection of that light shines into the dark places of this world, and the dark spaces in the hearts of people who inhabit it. With hope and grace we change some things and some people in accord with the way God works through our personal charisms.

At times our mirrors shine God's love brightly. Other times they appear jagged, cracked, dull or dirty. Each of us possesses this special reflective gift and how we pass it on to others depends on the qualities of our character and the mysteries of grace. Our physical finite beings are made up of many complex and intricate systems, yet none of them hold a candle to God's life in us. Through his life we become true bearers of his likeness in the world. God the Father is pure spirit. He remains invisible, almighty, eternal, incomprehensible, infinite, omnipotent and omnipresent. Yet, he relies on us to give flesh to his Spirit by bearing his image. This should give us cause for awesome reflections for the remainder of our lives.

So accustomed are we to our own image enhancements that we may miss the people and places that reflect God's image most brightly. God shines through those with simple faith and he reveals his power in those who are marginalized by society. There are people who can teach us how to love and trust. Somehow an old, worn-out body reveals the image of God more vividly than a well-muscled, youthful body.

The pride and dependence we have in ourselves can be dissipated as the weaknesses in our bodies becomes apparent. Tissues or organs that are flawed or diseased can become conduits that lead us to dependence on God. Our own superficial, transient glories fade as we find lasting peace and truly abide in the glory of God. It may be more difficult for people blessed with unusual beauty, intelligence and talent to develop a dependency on God. Those who are more gifted are also more challenged. Maintaining an attractive image that popular culture supports saps energy which could be used to uncover and build a true image of Jesus who lives within us. Our true image lies deep within us, its sacred location houses God's image and holds the essential ingredients for integrity of conscience. The journey inward takes ongoing effort, openness to graces in whatever forms they take, and a genuine appreciation of God's image in ourselves and others. Love inspires us to find God within and bring him out into the world through the appropriate use of our skills and aptitudes. God helps us to see with gentleness, listen with kindness, touch with compassion, think with mercy and speak with reassurance. Our bearing affects others for good or ill. A good example gives a greater impression than learned or clever eloquence. A good example is a fine speech we can make without saying a word. To walk the path of life uprightly may reform others unknowingly. Enthusiasm tempered with caution helps us share our gifts without either excess or deficiency.

Tempered enthusiasm helps us find the loving awareness of God's presence in every circumstance. Even if not markedly noticeable, it keeps us moving forward through thick and thin. With this awareness we can meet the challenges of life with a sustained fervor that is neither frenetic nor complacent. The positive energy that we find in tempered enthusiasm combines with our quest for goodness and truth. These forces keep us moving toward God. Negative energy generates if we dwell on present and future discouraging factors over long periods of time with a pessimistic attitude. Negative forces pull us away from God. One way people transform their environments is by the kind of energy they emit. Positive energy can revitalize humankind as negative energy can deteriorate all manner of life.

God's love recharges our positive energy when it is low and weakens our negative energy when it is of long standing. When God is the center of our lives and our universe, we become reflections of his love, just as the earth reflects the rays of the sun. We show the reality of God's love through actions that give life to the abstractions of our faith. The proper use of positive energy creates a force that stimulates the well-being of body, mind and soul. Although anger, conflict and stress may produce adverse physiological changes, faith, love and hope can bring strength to ourselves and our world.

The way we choose to direct our energies says much about who we are as individuals. We add quality energy to our immediate surroundings if we stay in the present moment. Considerable time spent dwelling or dreaming about the past or future is a waste of time. It also obliterates the present passage of time which could be put to use in a beneficial manner. To keep body, mind and soul together is an ongoing and difficult challenge. We cannot maintain unity or wholeness if one part of us is lagging in the past which is history, or galloping into the future which is mystery. Tender expressions of the service of love are as gifts of the present. We give them freely, without reflection on what has been or what might be.

One day a small boy surprised his father when he said: "I want to tell you something I have never told anyone before." "Tell me," said the father. He expected a secret about a friend, toy or school. "Love," said the child, "is something we need to take care of." Out of the mouths of babes comes wisdom beyond measure.

On the Formation of Goals

Dissatisfaction within a certain area of our lives may be the spark that ignites the fire for positive change. A vague sense of dissatisfaction may occur in any given area of our lives. This gnawing is not necessarily about what we are doing, but how we are experiencing life. A hard-working professional may have little time for personal hobbies. A wife and mother of several children may desire sound friendships with other women. A college student who lives in a noisy dorm may wish to develop his spiritual dimension. An older person who has a habit of asking others about what to do may want to strengthen his or her own decision-making qualities.

Often we can work through a vague dissatisfaction or trouble spot in a specific area of life with the passing of time. Self-knowledge, probing questions, valid information, wisdom from competent people, prayer and grace identify and address difficulties. Prudence and caution are beneficial when we search for people with whom we can confide. We can examine our values and desires in a specific area and put them into action by developing plans and practicing new techniques. Revisions are made until a workable pattern emerges. Changes usually happen slowly. The beginning stitches that emerge on fine embroidery look scattered and fragmented. However, the final product is well worth the effort. As we think about our goals, we should consider them as a means to an end. As we work toward them, we must avoid pushing away or taking advantage of people, or abusing or destroying things. It is good to set goals, but they should not be set in stone. We sew the embroidery of our lives by the performance of our daily activities. The strengths of the various threads symbolize the amount of love and creativity present in our actions. As we gather the cloth in our hands we can rework the design. The golden threads of God's graces and the multi-colored threads of our creative love join to form a very intriguing pattern. In the end, the finished product is one of unique beauty that will never be duplicated.

Several factors influence our choices in life. One of them is the use of pronouns. Most of the things we do, say, think or feel reflect how we view life and the world. People who commonly use I, me, or my, may have tunnel vision which focuses on their individual or immediate situations. The more people use these personal pronouns the smaller their world becomes. Because this perspective suggests considerable self-importance and self-preservation, these people desire to govern themselves with concrete laws, high competition, separatism and survival of the fittest. Their personal tactics may be arbitrary, insensitive and automatic. Isolation of humanity, one from another, and emphasis on success or failure reflects individual strengths and weaknesses and cause and effect. Self-serving choices support their ultra-independence and driving need for self-fulfillment. People who frequently use us, we, or our, may see humanity as a great family. The more people use these personal pronouns, the more they tend to give of themselves. Everyone connects with everyone else in one way or another. Each person is moving through the adventure of life, yet people are held together by their care for each other and by forces not yet understood. The maintenance of the interconnection between humans is accomplished through nurturing and being nurtured. A vision beyond individual, familial or local concerns sees global concerns as inextricably connected with those of the home front. Each person is responsible for the whole and affects the whole of creation. Energy from conflicts converts into energy for growth. Choices in this realm support mutual responsibility for the common good.

The pull of active and contemplative tensions also influences our behavior and decisions. Often our active needs depend on the success of our efforts to influence those around us. Similarly our contemplative needs depend on our inner resources, the most important of which are faith and love. These transforming active and contemplative forces vie for attention, nourishment and expression. Each has subtle nuances, significant movements and outstanding needs at different times in our lives. The tensions between action and contemplation will always be present. This is good and positive if we meet them with creativity and compassion. There is no precise point where the body stops and the mind begins, or where the mind stops and the soul begins; likewise with action and contemplation. There is no point where one stops and the other begins. Each gives life and growth to the other.

Our active and contemplative orientation is strengthened or weakened by two most generally known components in life, good and evil. The one that requires the most spiritual and mental combat is the downward pull of our fallen natures. This direction gains momentum from our individual and collective fears, violence, insecurities and all other manner of evil elements. Evil ranges from individual enticements to mob blatancy. It can influence our words and actions more than we realize. Evil can take place behind the closed doors of our families and communities. The evil of sin pulls us downward and discourages us by its massive injustice and indifference. Evil distorts or narrows our spiritual vision very quickly if we let our guard down or close off the spiritual pump. We should ever be on the watch for the devil who wears many disguises.

The upward pull of our redeemed nature helps us fight the battle with our fallen natures. Our belief in God's love keeps us undaunted by difficulties, oppression or opposition. Often latent faith emerges with determination that takes us beyond our own aspirations. We are people of God only to the degree in which we believe and trust in God, and actively allow him to transform us into the likeness of his Son. Our goodness shows that God exists in love and beauty.

The daily conscious choices we make reveal the essence of our Christian life which is God's love. The things we decide to do, how and for whom we do them, and the end results of our efforts embody that love. We transform ourselves and our environments to the degree in which we respond to boundless love in our various occupations. Some feedback about our activities come through our results and the reactions of others. This information, combined with insights from grace, indicates how others receive the visible actions of our love. Our potential for love is infinite. In our desire to give love to others we identify what it is that we want to do. Then we take the action necessary to accomplish whatever we identified, which usually fits within our abilities and talents. Our actions should be appropriate to our circumstances because we cannot give what we do not have. Love also calls us to explore new areas that stretch our creativity, or give up old activities so others may serve through them.

At times we may be challenged to make positive choices in an environment of evil negatives. An excellent example of this kind of choice was made by the Austrian psychiatrist Viktor Frankl. He was imprisoned at Auschwitz and other Nazi prisons for three years during World War II. His family was killed, but Doctor Frankl did not despair. He studied himself and his fellow prisoners and found that most people who held on to the hope of achieving something positive, even if it was the most mundane, survived. Hope keeps the inner spark of light burning when all outside is dark. Goals give our lives meaning and responsibility and express hope with a positive sense of purpose. We look forward and move toward that which gives us a reason to live. The slender threads of a broken life can be woven back together. Afterwards, the person gives strength and courage to others. The people we love, in union with our talents and our gift of faith, create beauty in the most vile of environments. They also keep us sane during seemingly intolerable times.

Gospel-based goals provide meaning for our efforts, motivation for our actions and direction for our sense of purpose. Our goals may be simple or complex, short or long term. Work goals may be delayed or may be changed over time. Christian goals give us ideals to work toward for a lifetime. A life without goals makes us lazy, complacent, confused, despondent or dispirited. As we strive toward realistic goals, we keep out of a rut and on the move. Receptivity to God's graces and sound discernment brings current goals to a reality or revises them, and formulates new goals for the future. Positive growth-producing goals motivate us through purposeful activities that transform our energy and time. We liberate ourselves from a rigid strategy and enjoy alternate possibilities toward meeting a goal. To enjoy an alert, forward thinking orientation until a goal is achieved, changed or abandoned has its own rewards.

Goals and roles change as we advance in years. We find challenges in career changes, family alterations, retirement options, health maintenance and spiritual quests. New possibilities and discoveries present themselves in every stage of adulthood and old age. However, too many possibilities and high expectations have disadvantages. Our options are available to the degree in which we are able to participate in them. Choosing what we can do depends on the availability of the activity, our energy level, time and money. Our energy and time might have to be channeled into responsibilities that we cannot neglect. There may be limits on our financial resources. Over-commitment or under-commitment in other areas of our lives need evaluation before we pursue anything new. We rarely achieve satisfaction by being the very best at most of the things we do. If expectations about how we ought to be are too high, too low, too many or too few, we risk burn-out or rust-out. Time is a good resource and we use it well when we neither rush to catch up or have large amounts of it on our hands. We enjoy the passing of time through effective planning and doing things reasonably well. It is noteworthy that even when we establish sound goals, the rhythm of change may bring some doubt and anxiety to our faith and hope.

A beautiful challenge available to each one of us is to be ourselves throughout our days. Sometimes we project false images of ourselves without realizing it. Instead, we must live the challenge of being ourselves because we know God loves us deeply. False pretenses, duplicities, show-time behavior and other traits that signal artificiality, build large barriers between us and true knowledge of ourselves. True self-knowledge keeps us right with God. John of the Cross connects us with our true selves with this advice: "Have a habitual desire to imitate Christ in all your deeds."

Days of Rest

A person will not be too far along on the spiritual road when he or she realizes the need for respite. Body, mind and soul yearn for it. Times of leisure, be it hours, days or weeks, balance the strain of doing a regular round of tasks and moving forward. Leisure activities offer challenge without stress, relaxing satisfaction, fresh ways of self-expression and natural restoration. As leisure diverts us from daily responsibilities, the things we do during recreation should bring lightsome refreshment our way. A catharsis may come from sports and exercise that require physical effort. Such strenuous activities may serve as a purgative and lift some of life's burdens from our shoulders. New knowledge may come about through leisure studies in any academic subject. These studies are relaxing because there are no performance evaluations, report deadlines or grades. Leisure learning has unexpected rewards. Social activities, from participating in good causes to travel cruises, offer many mind-broadening benefits. Each of us finds different kinds of satisfaction and contentment in the various recreational activities in which we participate. Regular breaks from our primary activities foster an increase in our creativity and productivity.

The humor we find in leisure lights up the rest of the day. It lessens grim associations connected to the work for which we are responsible because we can now find fun in our various tasks. Those of us who laugh easily usually get along well with others. We can find good-natured humor in almost anything, but most of all in ourselves. If we look closely at what we do, we find that anything can either strain or refresh us. How we do things determines how they affect us. We gain nothing if we grab to hoard things for ourselves, or hold things away from ourselves in a distant reserve. Leisure helps us laugh at ourselves, our idiosyncrasies and life. A day without a bit of laughter is a day of lamentation. Humor springs from love and shows harmony of the heart and soul. Our laughter shows that we enjoy our existence. A cheerful person makes his or her surroundings beautiful. Best of all a cheerful Christian is modest, peaceful, joyful and hopeful, which indicate a genuinely happy disposition. Laughter brings sunshine to the place where it is heard, because it rids the mind of dark cobwebs, sharp thistles and prickly cactus. "One word or a pleasing smile," said Thérèse of Lisieux, "is often enough to raise up a saddened and wounded soul." Good, overt expressions of leisure come from a mellow, interior continence which is calm, easy-going and at home in the presence of God. Leisure is much deeper than the things we do, holidays we celebrate or vacations we take. True leisure takes place in an inner space that is recollected and serene. Our leisure space helps us appreciate the many gifts that are ours to enjoy.

The best external space of leisure is like that which we find in a museum. A museum quiets us. It allows us to slow down. The displays are set apart so we can view them at our own pace. We may pass through the exhibits like a quick brown fox or stop and look at a snail's pace. The displays are available to look at in a restful milieu. The pace and environment of a museum greatly contrasts the pace and space of an international airport.

Many people live as if they reside in airports. Busy crowds give a high charge to the atmosphere. Quick movements and hurried activities set the pace as impulsive decisions and mechanical directions fill the space. Airport-like living is hazardous to long spiritual travels. It is better to board the museum shuttle, because this brief route called life is meant to be enjoyed. Hobbies, interests and just plain old fun help us put on the brakes and quiet our interior jets. If we really want to, we can live a peaceable life. Holy leisure teaches us that we do not need the hassle of a hectic world.

When they are channels for fun, leisure activities brighten our souls. To do something we have never done before can fire the imagination and perk creativity. Scribbles and random thoughts may offer intriguing interpretations. Writing a poem or drawing a tree may reveal wondrous abilities or giggles. Whittling, whistling or building a red wagon may become absorbing and fascinating. New leisure adventures keep the fun-loving parts of ourselves alive. Leisure tasks are neither highly organized nor competitive. A lovely leisure finds expression in the natural play of children. So we sing a funny song, have a teddy bear picnic, explore rocks on the shore, build sand castles or watch the storm clouds without being self-conscious. We take a walk without going anywhere, pet a furry friend, eat a piece of pie or imagine being a tree in the wind, with a free spirit. To experience leisure activities with childlike wonder is to loosen up and enjoy the graces of serendipity.

For many who have an interest in sports, that interest is often vicarious. We are spectators. Watching others play is like reading about the experiences of saints and heroes. The experiences are inspirational and adventuresome, but at a safe distance from us. Achieving satisfaction through the efforts of others seems somewhat limiting in the long run. If we are truly impressed by someone else's virtue or courage, we should do likewise. Each of us is capable of unique expressions of ourselves. No one can be a better us than us.

A wide range of involvement is open to us if we show interest in a particular sport. Interest may range from "I must make the team," to "This sport gives me a spiritual tingle." We may pound a bouncing ball with a competitive vengeance or see it as a backdrop that gives rhythm to the simple flow of life. The rhythm of a bouncing ball in tennis, a bobbing float in fishing or the pattern in snow made by a cross country skier brings an increased awareness of the activity with a decreased awareness of the performance. With that focus, skill levels are placed in the background and the activity is enjoyed because of the components that hold it together.

The possibilities for leisure are endless, limited only by our imagination and creativity. We can enjoy or appreciate watching nature, people, and grand or insignificant events alone or with others. Creativity can be expressed in photography, painting or various crafts. We can stimulate our intellect through lectures, current events, collecting and reading. Physical exercise can be enjoyed in team sports or yoga, or we can relax alone by listening to music.

Music has been called the language of the soul. Depending on the type of music we like, listening can be deeply relaxing or highly energizing. Leisure listening allows us to get lost in the music since we need not critique or analyze it. Music alters the body, mind and soul. Loud or harsh sounds can injure our ear drums, set our nerves on edge or shred our soul. Soft, soothing sounds enhance relaxation, stimulate the imagination and send gentle vibrations to our soul. They are also capable of stirring the emotions and memories. We experience this at weddings, graduations and funerals. In every culture, music accompanies spiritual or religious ritual. From the rousing drum beat of a tribal dance to the mournful strains of a medieval requiem, music is a part of us. Its influence ennobles or subdues us.

Leisure is best when we do not force it, but let it move within to harmonize our lives. Leisure lets us poke around and take our time, and is the best of carefree times. If there are no worries about doing things right, poking around gives us unexpected pleasures. We can enjoy things without owning them. We relish the feeling of a cool breeze on a warm day, or listening to and watching the waves on a lake. Leisure in life is like a voyage on a schooner. We can enjoy the view, explore the ship, make friends with the captain, talk a bit, eat a bit, fish a little and then get off when we get home. The trip was wonderful because we did not own the boat, buy it, control what happened or get stuck on it. We did not have to make something happen. We just enjoyed our time as it meandered by. Creativity is what we do when we have nothing to do. We can hold it down with sleep, mindless TV or empty talk, or can stimulate it by doing something we have never done before. Although an industry has been built around various kinds of leisure, we know very little about its substance. Leisure is more about something we feel on the inside, than about something we do on the outside. Good leisure makes us better persons. It nourishes the body, mind and soul by renewing and refreshing our lives. It is definite substance in our quest for holiness. Prayerfulness and playfulness are very close. Playful people of prayer radiate a joyful enthusiasm about life. True leisure is relaxing, revitalizing and fascinating. It is true that God rested on the seventh day, and sometimes we wonder what he did.

To Live as Resurrection

Past occurrences, both positive and negative, influence our orientation toward the world. Peace and contentment will be ours, no matter what the past, if we keep a resurrection outlook uppermost in our minds and hearts. The view from a resurrection orientation focuses more on love, beauty and forgiveness. We remain aware of the effects of indifference, injustice and sin, but do not let them overwhelm us. One way to make sense out of our confusing world is to love it. God is where love is and we come to know God better as we learn to love the unexplainable more. As pilgrims on the move, we can strive to love deeper, better and more, as we grow in integrity, wisdom and grace. Authentic love gives more quality and depth to our daily lives than anything else we see or do. If we are able to find quiet love and uplifting grace in something quite ordinary, we can sustain a contemplative demeanor. A baby's face, a refreshing scent in the air, a flowering or dead bush, ants working, sunlight streaming through a window, or a tree in the yard may become magical for a few moments. They lift us out of the commonplace into the extraordinary through a simple glance. A moment of special grace is like a soft touch amid the hard shoves of life. A contemplative demeanor is one of presence, with a gentle and tender receptivity in times of peace or confusion. Moments of grace are often silent and supernatural.

Finding a few sweet moments in our days neutralizes the harsh realities in our lives. A light touch of grace brings wholeness to brokenness, loving attention to the immediate and the affirmation of a trusting and hopeful outlook. As we live resurrection in a world that is constantly crucified, we learn the importance of little things that are life-giving. We express resurrection every day in small, homey ways. Writing a letter or making a phone call just to express care, tilting the head in silent loving recognition, extending an affirming touch and listening from the heart are very small things that encourage life. Indeed, there are many unobtrusive ways to grace the world with new life.

When days become a scramble, and one hurtful or vexing thing follows another without rhythm or reason, we must hold on in trust and try not to lose our inner vision of resurrection. As the trapeze artist catches his partner in flight, so do we stretch out our arms for Jesus to catch us and pull us to safety. In flight, with outstretched arms, we trust Jesus will be there for us. We trust against trust that he will pull us out of our trials and troubles, especially when solutions seem so very elusive.

Resurrection harmony exists within the body, mind and soul, as we live it with meaning, in beauty and trust. Because of this, we can be lifted above the merciless conditions we experience and observe. We are not overwhelmed by the grime of the world, nor do we live with our heads in the celestial clouds of the world to come. Resurrection means living the heights of our vision while giving loving attention to the world around us.

Our Christian faith takes us beyond the confusing and frustrating events of the past and present. We know we are not helpless victims tossed around by storm waves in life's ocean. The combination of resources in our body, mind and soul are stronger and more resilient than we think. Small changes for the good help us find our true selves in Jesus. While growth in Christ is gradual, it usually takes place in fits and starts at the least expected times. Our actions come from trust in God, responsibility to self and a greater appreciation of others. Small changes for the greater good have a ripple effect in the lives around us. Yes, mountains can be moved, one rock at a time.

Our minds and souls contain a strange mix of virtues and vices, good and evil, imperfections and gifts, bad habits and good traits. Sometimes it seems as if everything negative rises to the surface and wreaks havoc with our resurrection orientation. We may bring many of our problems on ourselves by sinking our own little boat when we do something without considering the implications that will follow our action. If we do not know what to do, sometimes we may not do anything. The *Titanic* was a large ship and was not supposed to sink. There were many people on board who did not get into the lifeboats. Subsequently there were two hundred empty seats in those lifeboats. We too can be so cautious that we do not do what common sense tells us we should do. God does not specifically tell us what to do because it would violate his gift of choice to us. Trust in God takes us beyond our own perceptions when life does not make sense, and confirms that a quality life is founded on integrity of the soul.

The signs and effects of original sin appear in many forms. At times life seems quite absurd. We experience financial collapse. We lose our jobs or homes. We are stabbed in the back then abandoned by friends. We sustain a catastrophic injury or disfiguring disease. During these times we go to prayer. Empty and desolate, we avoid telling God what we want him to do or even what we want. We rest in the assurance that he is there with us and will not abandon us. Having no idea what to think or do, we only trust with a stark, raw faith and through prayer give God the freedom to bring good out of evil. Such is living the resurrection while on earth. When life is uncertain and the shifting sands of structures move under our feet, we lean on the providence of God, live prayer and hold on to gospel values. During difficult and confusing times we find consolation as we reflect on Teresa's familiar words:

> Let nothing disturb you.
> Let nothing frighten you.
> For all things pass save God
> Who does not change.
> Be patient and at the last
> You will find
> All fulfillment.
> Hold God and nothing
> Will fail you,
> For he alone is all.

Our mistakes and failures teach us that there are always ingredients for growth in any negative that comes our way. Even though our capacity for sin is very much with us, we can still strive to push ahead on our spiritual path because the best lessons we learn can come from our mistakes, failures and sins. However, we need not dwell on them for long, realizing that at times defeat is a first step to something better. We risk failure when we go that extra mile, forage into the unknown or do things differently. Self-fulfilling prophecy suggests that if we think in a failure mode, with "It won't work" or "It cannot be done" as mottoes, there will be failure. If we think in a mode of blessings, we will become blessings. The human body is quite a precious and vulnerable specimen as it reacts to thoughts and talk. Negative communication wears it down and positive communication builds it up. We can confirm a culture of life by a positive outlook or negate it by complaints. To hold a positive, resurrection vision of life in our hearts and minds brings benediction to ourselves and others.

Our character is shaped by our inner consistency, values, ethics, morals, integrity and spiritual beliefs. It is stretched and reshaped by the cumulative choices we make throughout our lifetime. Most choices are small and mundane and we make them almost automatically. On the other hand, some decisions are difficult and require serious prayer, reflection and patience. However, it is hard to be patient when we are in a hurry, and hard to forgive when we are deeply hurt. We find difficulty in showing interest if we are bored, speaking the truth when it might cause pain, or being silent about the confidences we hold. It is not easy to remain faithful when we are strongly tempted, or to think things through rather than act on impulse. Natural impulses can pull us toward greed rather than generosity, and can cause us to pout rather than pray. Yet pray we must, and through it we reform our lives.

When we have tried every way we know to solve a problem but have not been successful, it is time to stop, sit back, say a slow *Our Father* and continue doing the best we can. Blessed are we when we see the clouds of our sorrows as God's protective wings. Blessed are we who slowly realize this, even if it may take the good part of a lifetime. Blessed are we when we reach some degree of resignation over problems that have no solutions, or questions that have no answers. As we look down the centuries of time, we often find it is suffering that motivated the work of artists and saints.

The harmony and unity of our bodies, minds and spirits increase or decrease by how we do things, from self-care tasks all the way to prayer. Harmony is in tune when people who live together are not influenced by the rapid or stagnating pace of society. Harmony occurs when the people who live together become aware of their speed as a unit. They work as a group to maintain that pace even when pressure from the outside dictates a different pace. Activities that flow evenly enrich and nourish the environment in ways we cannot comprehend. Harmony makes departures and returns to the household easier to handle. A prayerful harmony is expressed through the love, care and attention we give to household chores. Harmony is maintained when each person in the house knows what is going on, when things are going to happen, where the people are and what is expected of each person. Harmony within a home helps the people who live there feel calm and serene. Moderate TV, radio and appliance noise, brief phone calls, good organization, quiet times and quiet voices enhance the peace in the house. Because the foundation of harmony is prayer, neglecting or substituting the best of good works for prayer dilutes it. People who live under the same roof are in harmony when they take household responsibilities seriously. This includes many small considerations. Telephone messages are accurate and delivered promptly. All practice the Golden Rule. Each tries to remain rational and calm during disputes. Name calling, accusations or sulking are kept to a minimum. A mature person takes responsibility for his or her feelings and behavior rather than ascribing what has happened to external events or other people. He or she knows how words can be used to flatter, obscure, enlighten, confuse, charm, accuse, reveal or conceal, but instead seeks the forthright approach. Words have the power to ignite wars or promote peace. Clear words in simple phrases hold beauty which can banish doubt while revealing deep thoughts and feelings.

Local harmony that sustains day to day activities enhances

universal harmony. Late at night, when all is quiet, one can feel the slow, regular pulse of life within a home where harmony prevails. The nightly cessation of activities leads to a deeper rhythm of body, mind and spirit. Such a rhythm merges into the natural cadence one finds in nature. The change of seasons, the pull of the moon on the tides, the wind on the waves, the breezes in the trees blend in sweet harmony. Even though vibrations from man-made noises such as traffic, machines, industry and sirens spoil the rhythm of nature, somehow beautiful, unknown graces draw all of creation into the ceaseless rhythm of God's love. A person's way of talking, listening, thinking, breathing, loving and praying are unique and express his or her way of being. To see each person as changing and growing toward a greater good reflects a viable body, mind and soul. An individual moves into personal development and growth within the groups of which he or she is a part. The manifestation of growth is harmonic when it is simultaneously within the self and the other, in the I and the thou. The fruitfulness of each individual encompasses family and community harmony. If people think only of their own fulfillment, they become deaf to the music around them. Solo players without accompaniment limit their ability to share their talents by not supporting a greater good. To sing one's own song distances an individual from the supportive harmony he or she could find in the chorus of life. A soloist emerges to perform and then disappears to join again with the orchestra.

Life as we know and experience it on the physical plane is a small part of our spiritual journey. We are members of the great family of God. Life is infinitely connected to our deceased friends and family from generations gone by, to saints and blesseds whom we did not know on earth, and to all who are yet to be born and received into God's family on earth. We are as links in a chain bonded by grace beyond our understanding. In the steps of those hearty Christians who trod before us, we learn that the more we personally mature the more we share the responsibilities of others. Because it takes us beyond feelings and efforts to true commitments of long standing, love passes through infatuations and honeymoons. It thrives in time and is tried in the furnace of sacrifice. Love brings us to prayer. We cannot survive in this world, nor expect new life in the next, without a strong prayer life.

Physically we are vulnerable to death and decay. Yet, death is much more than the termination of our vital signs. Death sets our souls free to live forever. The dying and death of others can impart to us its own wisdom. It is indeed true that love is stronger than death. Love survives and may even continue to grow after the shock of the sudden loss of a loved one softens. Although we cannot see our departed loved ones in heaven, we can communicate with them through our prayers.

The Triune God, Father, Son and Holy Spirit, shows us how love unites a family. We become a part of God's eternal family by Baptism and live our lives by loving and listening to him. God is nearer to us than we know and he always wants us to be close to him. We grow in his life and love as we walk with grace through this valley of tears and smiles. Then we pass through the thin veil of death. The blossoms of love we give in this world will reach full flower in the world to come. Love reaches perfection as we experience the divine essence in the beatific vision. At that time, we will be fully embraced by the glorious wonder of God. At long last, we will experience the fulfillment of our deepest human longings.

May we return to our Creator who formed us from the dust of the earth. May Mary, the angels and all the saints come to meet us as we go forth from this life. May joy beyond all measure be ours as we finally see Jesus, our redeemer, face to face.

7

Stewards of Conservation

Love people even in their sin, for that is the semblance of divine love and is the highest love on earth. Love all of God's creation, the whole and every grain of sand of it. Love every leaf, every ray of God's light. Love the animals, love the plants, love everything. If you love everything, you will perceive the divine mystery in things. Once you perceive it, you will begin to comprehend it better every day. And you will come at last to love the whole world with an all-embracing love.   *Dostoyevsky*

The life and teachings of John of the Cross are of universal interest because they speak to the deepest aspirations of every person. John's poems, like metaphysical fires, explain the wonders of God through Jesus, the Church, the mystery of prayer and the majesty of God's creation. John was spellbound by the wonders of God's beauty found on mother earth. He was utterly in awe of the splendor of God's gifts, be it flowers by day or stars by night. One of his favorite activities was to go on long hikes with his confreres. John spent days on the hillsides where he basked in the beauties of flora and fauna. Nature kindled John's burning love for God. While he sat under a tree, he penned these words: "Scattering a thousand graces he passed through these groves in haste, and left them with his glance alone, clothed in beauty."

An old story is told about a teacher who gathered his students together very early in the morning, before the dawn. It was still quite dark and he told them to pay attention because he had a very important question to ask: How could they tell when night had ended and day had begun? One student replied: "Could it be when you see an animal and can tell whether it is a sheep or a dog?" "No," said the teacher. Another student replied: "Could it be when you look at a tree in the distance and can tell whether it is a fig tree or a peach tree?" "No," answered the teacher. After a few more guesses the students said: "Tell us sir, what is it?" The teacher replied, "It is when you look into the face of any man or woman and see that he is your brother or she is your sister. If you cannot do this, no matter what time it is, it will still be night."

The first time we approach people from different cultures, religions or countries, we should, symbolically or literally, take off our shoes. This approach should remind us that God was there before our arrival and is still present. That illumination keeps us from treading on the histories or dreams of others, or forcing our ways of thinking or of doing things into their heads. One reality that should remain with us through our entire lives is that we all belong to God. One race or culture is not superior to another.

An important measure of civilization within a race or culture is how they treat their children, elderly and marginalized members. God is Father to all and blesses us with his creative gifts. Animals, plants, fruits and vegetables are ours to share, not to stockpile. A sacred attitude in life and toward life comes forth as we gather the fruits of mother earth according to need, and care for the productive capacities of the earth with gratitude. There is enough for our need but not for our greed. If we live simply, others may simply live.

Pope John Paul II said: "Today the dramatic threat of ecological breakdown is teaching us the extent to which greed and selfishness — both individual and collective — are contrary to the order of creation.... An education in ecological responsibility is urgent; responsibility for oneself, for others and for the earth.... A true education in responsibility entails a genuine conversion in ways of thought and behavior."

Our present and future relationship with the land should reflect the sacred wisdom of the native Americans. They have always known that human beings are a part of nature. Because of this, Indians respect the young as individuals in their own right, the old for their wisdom, and the earth for its bounty and fragility. Within many Indian societies people are not valued for what they own, but for what they give away. Those who give generously, without regard to cost, are most admired.

Among the Lakota tribe, weddings, births, funerals and other important events were accompanied by an 'otuhan,' which was a time to give away possessions. The family of the bride, or the new parents, gave away many things that they owned or made in order to celebrate the special event. No one went without because the people who gave would receive at the next 'otuhan.' Exceptional generosity was the primary way by which status and prestige were gained within the Indian tribe. Indians often gave away their food, clothing and horses to those in need so everyone had enough.

Among the Lakota and other northern plains Indians, circles of life within nature are found in abundance and deeply revered. The sun, moon, earth and planets are round. The circular flow of day and night and the four seasons ceaselessly come and go. Circles mark the age of trees and are the forms of seeds and fruits. Circular housing ranges from the small nests of birds to large tepees. Tepees were often placed in a circle when a tribe set up camp. To the Indian a circle imparted unity as symbolized in togetherness when sitting around a campfire and in each family circle. Just as the family is a part of the larger tribal circle, so each nation is a part of the world. In the great circle of life, each individual comes from God, lives, dies and returns to God.

Circles are a symbolic part of reality. They express harmony in life and nature. In a circle no one is first or last. Circles are within, over and under other circles, and also symbolize the eternity of God. They are timeless and even bring new life from death.

Circles of grace find gain in loss, breakthrough in breakdown and stepping stones in stumbling blocks. The journey of a human life is an upward spiral if one stays on the spiritual path. Grace softens movement around the hard curves of life and appears when there is need of rising again to life. Each ending connects with a new beginning, just as dawn follows darkness.

The circle is found in some American Indian cultures again and again. In their dances, art, beliefs and life, everything connects to everything else. All people, all nature and the Maker of all are united. No matter where one goes or what one becomes that individual is still a part of his or her circles of life. To live with reverence in these circles is to uphold the structure, experience and sacredness of family and community life. Chief Seattle is believed to have said: "All things are bound together, all things connect. What happens to the earth, happens to the children of the earth. Man has not woven the web of life, he is but one thread. Whatever he does to the web, he does to himself."

Some spiritual wisdom of the American Indian is expressed in the following prayer by Yellow Lark, Sioux Indian Chief: "Oh Great Spirit, whose voice I hear in the winds, whose breath gives life to all the world, hear me. I come before you as one of your many children. I am small and weak. I need your strength and wisdom. Let me walk in beauty and make my eyes ever behold the red and purple sunset. Make my hands respect the things you have made. My ears sharp to hear your voice. Make me wise so that I may know the things to teach my children, the lessons you have hidden in every leaf and rock. I seek strength not to be superior to my brothers, but to be able to fight my greatest enemy — my pride. Make me ever ready to come to you with clean hands and clear eyes. And when life fades as a fading sunset, let my spirit come to you without shame. Amen"

Spirituality and beauty were so intertwined in the daily life of the American Indian that no words separated them. English equivalents cannot define them. The world of the spirit, human

relationships, beauty and the commonplace of routine were like
mirrors that reflected a deeper reality of each in the minds and
hearts of the Indians. They did not create objects of art for the
sake of art. Neither art nor beauty were distinct from life. For them
there was not much difference between praying and dancing. Daily
life and spiritual practices were present in rituals and ceremonies.
Everything was sacred through great reverence for the earth, sky,
air and all elements of life. Because the sacred realm was present
in everything, the only time something became profane was when
someone turned away from the sacred path. The sacredness of life
had to be claimed over and over again.

Most Indians cherished the land beyond its monetary value
because they viewed themselves as sacred caretakers. A oneness
with the universe and all powers made all life sacred. All were
brothers and sisters. An aesthetic vision of the universe and the
functional aspects of Indian culture were as one. Baskets, cradle
boards and bowls displayed high levels of detail and craftsmanship
and were used for daily needs. The possessions Indians had were
few: survival tools, religious objects, clothing, cooking and eating
utensils, objects for child rearing, horses and a dwelling. Indians
used the buffalo for food, clothing, tools and fuel. The earth and
its creatures were part of the Indian, just as the Indian was part
of the earth. Everything and everyone was holy. All belonged to
the same family. Most American Indians were excellent stewards
of the land. We can learn much from them.

God creates and loves what he has created. God the Son
became incarnate, one with humankind. When Jesus redeemed the
world through the cross, it became a mysterious sign of great love.
The center of the cross is paradox, since it is the heart of collision
and contradiction, as well as a place of meeting, change and unity.
The cross symbolizes the best gifts of life and the worst experiences
of death, and both never seem to be far from each other.

Jesus continues to show his everlasting love for us through
the Eucharist. Wheat and grapes, gifts from the earth, become

the body and blood of Jesus, God's greatest gift to us. Everything connects in the body of Christ, as the last verses of the sequence of Corpus Christi illustrate: "Jesus, good shepherd and true bread, have mercy on us. May you feed and protect us; May you lead us to see good things in the land of the living. You, who know and can do all things; You who feed us mortals now, make us banquet as coheirs and friends with you and the saints of the holy city." Our relationship with the earth is one of stewardship. As with the American Indians who gave us the practice of stewardship par excellence, it is our sacred duty to pass on an intact environment to the next generation, and they to pass it on to the generations to come. What we do, or fail to do, to the environment now will have its effect on how we experience eternity in the future.

On the Mercy of God

Mercy is the fruit of compassion. We feel compassion in sympathetic thoughts toward the distress others experience. We find the existence of the compassion of God in the compassion of humankind. Our compassion toward those whom we touch exhibits care and understanding. Compassion reminds us that justice is essential for all people.

Compassion is put into action by numerous forms of mercy. Mercy moves compassion into a practical mode with energy that comes from a readiness and willingness to help others. As William Shakespeare wrote: "The quality of mercy is not strained. It droppeth as the gentle rain from heaven upon the place beneath. It is twice blest. It blesseth him that gives and him that takes." A small drop of mercy can be a saving grace.

The universal essence of mercy is forgiveness. Mercy reaches out to those in need with compassionate eyes and warm hands. Since mercy comes from the heart of God, she helps us see him in each person, no matter how wretched the person may be. Every person has a soul with an eternal destiny. Mercy gives us courage and strength. With the merciful Jesus, we encounter various wretched situations in the world. With him we become gentle and kind when we are with others. With him we strive to be true in speech, just in judging, competent in business, close to the land and respectful of all that is around us.

The psalmist wrote that God's mercy endures forever. God is most gracious, slow to anger, ready to pardon and of great kindness. Kindness, as with all good things, originates in God and is like a loving chain that links humanity together. Before we can be merciful and kind to others, we need to be merciful and kind to ourselves. How do we do this? We are kind to ourselves in a firm way by neither spoiling nor pampering ourselves. Conversely, we are kind when we do not overextend ourselves to the point of destroying our unique personhood. We should give what we have with prudence, by firmly channeling our unique goodness and gifts in life-enriching directions. We persevere in kindness as long as we respect the rights of all peoples and wisely use the resources of the earth. Each is dependent on the other. One area of respect cannot stand alone. A ruinous imbalance occurs in an individual who plants young trees to restore a forest, but supports or participates in the abortion of unborn children.

As we grow older, our physical and mental health decline. We begin our development at conception and enjoy the fastest rate of growth between conception and birth. The miracle of life is most amazing during these nine months. If conservation is respect for humanity and the wise use of everything on the earth for a lasting good, then conservation is only possible as long as we affirm life. The good of humankind develops from reverence for humankind. Human development is at its peak during gestation. Conception and subsequent maturation in utero is the greatest wonder in the world. Therefore, destruction of life in the womb violates the very heart of conservation.

The transition from life in the womb to life in the world is indeed traumatic and awesome. As we mature, we all develop personal behavior patterns which support or oppose, in varying degrees, Christian tenets. The lasting good in humanity begins with ourselves and the decorum to which we ascribe. However, proper decorum is not the absolute sign of Christian witness. It is one of several attributes that enables growth in Christian formation. Gospel values give grace, propriety, tact and responsibility to what we say and do. The expression of good manners are a part of our Christian uniqueness. Sound respect for others, especially the very young and the very old, spreads harmony throughout humanity. Respect for ourselves goes hand in glove with respect for others, as both are sound signs of love because their manifestations are compatible with growth in holiness and wholeness. Love for ourselves, others and God goes beyond talk to labors of mind and heart.

We show self-respect through a neat and clean appearance, unassuming dress, correct speech, good posture, personal hygiene and tidy living environment. Social respect is shown through polite manners, with the frequent use of "please" and "thank you." By using a light touch rather than a heavy hand, we utilize common goods gratefully and respectfully. Social respect is expressed by not keeping borrowed items longer than necessary and returning calls promptly. We also mind our own business, even if we have inquiring minds and want to know. An overly curious person may resemble a busybody. Busybodies are always on the move as they cannot control their desires to see with roving eyes who walks by, comes in, or goes out. Their ears are like radar that catches every word said. It is easy to see how this type of sensory input depletes personal and social respect.

Personal and social respect bring insight and sensitivity to our world. Because of respect we become accustomed to thinking about what effect our words or behavior may have on others. Forethought may avoid tensions that our behavior might cause, since it places attention on actions that might cause embarrassment or pain to others. Also, forethought before making a promise warns us not to make it if we cannot keep it. Thinking ahead says we leave things as we would like to find them. We automatically fill the gas tank or juice container for the next person, and hope this practice may rub off on others. Most of all, we preserve the dignity of others by not pressing them with our unsolicited advice, opinions, tastes or philosophies. Instead, our thoughts, so urgently in need of expression, are put on hold by finding our strength in the love we give away to others. We ourselves change, not for the sake of change, but because change takes our steps closer to Jesus.

A Matter of Conscience

We cannot change the collective conscience of humanity for the better unless we achieve a transformation of conscience as individuals. The ethics and values of our public lives are sound when they support the intrinsic dignity and inalienable rights of each person. Each of us is inescapably responsible for what we do or do not do. Our individual deeds, omissions, decisions and failures have consequences that ripple through our global community and change its collective consciousness. Positive transformation of the collective consciousness is possible through the awakening and growth of individual spiritual renewal and conscience reform.

The truth is often obscure in our society. An accurate view concerning what is going on around us is not easy to obtain. Verbal engineers take ugly things and wrap them in nice language so that they sound like something else. An example is "pro choice." Although this term sounds positive, it negates the lives of those who are defenseless. The primary asset in the discovery of truth is a heightened perception of what constitutes the quality of life and the forces that enhance or demean life. We find truth within the light of God's providence. Conscience formation takes place as we apply specific knowledge to concrete moral situations. A moral decision in a present circumstance will either subscribe to something that will be done for the good, or will be avoided or changed because it is evil.

Many people take pride in forming their own consciences, but in view of what? It would be interesting to conduct a survey regarding what elements form the consciences of such individuals. Perhaps we would hear responses such as: the latest trends in society, the media, civil laws, advice columnists, movie stars, teachers, talk show hosts, theologians or gurus. To let one's conscience be one's guide is not necessarily the wisest of ways in which to go. The decisions of conscience are a product of the better self, so long as there is a better self with which to go. Many people are good, thoughtful, and patient. Their identity may be formed by familial or cultural guidelines. There may be vague associations to God, but no spiritual life. People can also build their conscience identity on the passing opinions of modern thinkers or popular heroes. Conscience can have many sources for development.

Freedom of choice can be like an unguided missile unless it is grounded in truth and aimed at the greater good. The viability of a society lies not in power or wealth, but in spiritual roots that form stable marriages and decent family life. Conscience choices that support strong families are essential because societies will eventually self-destruct without traditional families. People who choose to live virtuous, spiritually based lives within a society give it more credibility than efficient operations or state of the arts systems.

Every choice has a price. The concepts of right, wrong, good or bad go beyond individual choice or thought. People cannot do what is objectively wrong without facing the consequences, now or later. People who consistently choose the wrong can easily sway from high moral codes and become completely at home in corrupt life styles. The intellect can be altered, bit by bit, until it is no longer in harmony with Christian teachings. Many keep the letter of the law, but willfully violate its spirit. The penalty of consistent wrongdoing is in a dead conscience. A conscience of this type may never have known or have slowly regressed from the basic concept of right or wrong. Unfortunately those with dead consciences get significant coverage in the news media.

Now ascending the scale a little, we can find people with consciences that are half-baked. This type of conscience may be immature or uninformed, because the information that is present may be inaccurate or incomplete. If resources for conscience development are available, and an individual does not utilize them, the half-baked state is a result of choice. Indifference or indolence are present in every area of existence. A third type of conscience is quite common, and is of the Swiss cheese variety. It resembles a cafeteria meal of pick and choose, with no consistency in nourishment or content. These people believe what they want because they select what they like and leave custom-made holes in basic beliefs. Since God is made in their own image and likeness, these people believe whatever strikes their fancy at the moment. When certain subjects appear that make these people uneasy, the subjects are changed, dropped or avoided. Often Swiss cheese people follow their own conscience. Woe to them if they extend this practice to the rules of the road.

The sincere conscience group has many members. How can they be wrong if they are sincere? On the contrary these people only kid themselves into thinking they are true to their consciences. The question is, what are the truths their consciences are based upon and on what do they base these truths? Sincere does not mean virtuous or upright since individuals can easily be sincere and foolish, sincere and weak, sincere and wrong. Because it can be relatively simple to delude oneself and others, a person can fail to act on what is right. In time a person can come to judge whatever he or she does is right. People can be sincere seekers of truth but, if their truth is not grounded in Scripture, it can be flawed. No one is exempt from the effects of original sin. People can be sincere and do incredibly evil things, as the history of humanity can attest. Since people can be sincerely correct or sincerely mistaken, illogical or misleading, it is easy for them not to fault themselves under almost any circumstances. There is so much "no fault" and as much hurt and loose ends because of it.

Conscience has need of guidance since it is not infallible. We can almost drown out the voice of God with the noise of voices from ourselves and others. No one has the right to form his or her morality independently of the will of God. Conscience has been called a little spark of celestial fire which we must labor to keep alive, and indeed, this is so.

As Catholics we are highly blessed with the soundest of guides on all essential points of conscience formation and Christian doctrine. We form and reform our consciences according to the principles revealed by God in Sacred Scripture. These principles are clarified by sacred tradition which is taught by the Church in the name of Jesus, under the guidance of the Holy Spirit. The basic teachings of the Catholic Church, the repository of truth through the centuries, have withstood the test of time. From this repository we make decisions and practical judgments about the many facets of daily living. The strength of our Catholic heritage gives us a firm identity. We apply, with certitude, moral knowledge and wisdom to subjective decisions, ethical proprieties and specific actions. To act with a doubtful conscience is the same as shooting first and asking questions later. That is why it is better to resolve doubt by getting answers from experts with well-formed consciences. We continue to ask questions until we reach a point of practical certitude which resolves doubts. Then our actions should be subjectively certain and objectively correct. Like muscles or skills, we strengthen our virtues by use. Conversely, they can weaken or atrophy through neglect. Virtues help our wills, desires, thoughts, feelings and judgments to work together toward sound applications. Virtues help us arrive at solid moral decisions with greater ease. Indeed, our faith is a gift which transforms our prayer, data and intellectual conclusions into convictions.

We should not confuse good with nice. Upon noticing a well-groomed, well-dressed, courteous, attractive person, how easy it is for us to incorporate moral virtues into these endowments. The tendency is strong to confuse what is beautiful, successful and nice with what is moral and good. A successful person or a societal hero may or may not be a virtuous person. There were well-mannered men who were devotees of Beethoven and Bach and connoisseurs of the graphic arts. They also ordered and participated in the extermination of millions of people in the Nazi concentration camps. Today, well-spoken, friendly and refined medical personnel also terminate life. Appearances are so deceiving and it is quite possible to do good or be nice without God. As Paul wrote in First Corinthians 13:1, "If I speak in human and angelic tongues, but do not have love, I am a resounding gong or a clashing cymbal." Love is rooted in loving God for himself. Often appearances impress us, but God always sees what is in the heart. Unfortunately, original sin introduced ambivalence and indifference into human affairs. However, even though we share in a fallen world, we also partake in the beauty of the heavenly city. Godly features in our earthly city will form part of our heavenly realm. Our lives express true value and virtue as long as we stick with God and attribute our value and virtue to him.

The restoration of natural creation mirrors the marvels of the Creator. God wills to share his creative power with humankind. The Church militant is made up of men and women who live in the earthly city. We constitute a variety of people who differ in race, language and nationality, as we strive to live in a civil manner by enriching one another. Together, as a people, we find God in truth and serve him in holiness. There is nothing of worth that will not endure if we love God.

Gaudium et Spes (#39), the *Pastoral Constitution on the Church in the Modern World*, a document of Vatican Council II, advises us: "Although earthly progress must be sedulously distinguished from the growth of Christ's kingdom, nevertheless, inasmuch as it is able to contribute to a more human society, such progress is of very great importance to the Kingdom of God. The goods of human dignity, fraternal union, and liberty, that is all these goods of nature and the fruits of human industry, after we have produced them on earth in the spirit of the Lord and according to his command, we will find again later on, but cleansed from all stain and illumined and transfigured when Christ gives back to his Father the eternal and universal kingdom, a 'kingdom of truth and life, a kingdom of holiness and grace, a kingdom of justice, love and peace.' Already the kingdom is present in mystery on earth; it will be completed when the Lord comes."

We build this good, earthly city of ours with the mortar of friendship. Friendship is the foundation stone for marriage and family. In order to be friends, we must honor truth. Francis de Sales notes: "For those who dwell in the world and desire to embrace true virtue, it is necessary to unite themselves together by a holy and sacred life. By this means they encourage, assist and conduct one another to good deeds."

The insights of true friends are more useful than the good will of acquaintances. Rare and beautiful is a friendship without self-interest. Its bedrock is responsibility, not opportunity. Friendships that last require continual mutual respect. An impulse that leads us to a friend may be God's light which guides us to a new adventure. Friendship grows slowly but surely as it withstands and passes through the shocks of adversity.

Each person is a member of the human race, therefore a social being. He or she possesses the power of influence and natural good. When these two elements combine with the practice of virtue, authentic friendships can be sustained. We cultivate sound friendships with care and prayer. In his *Confessions*, Augustine describes the fruits of friendship: "There is a wide range of things that captivate the soul in friendships: Conversing and laughing together, mutually complying with one another in good will, reading the same books and discussing them pleasantly, wasting time together or spending it seriously, disagreeing at times without rancor as one disagrees with oneself, solidifying the very many agreements by that very rare disagreement, mutually teaching and learning from each other, bothered by a desire for absent friends and welcoming their return with joy. By these things and by signs of this type that are like kindling wood, souls are forged together and made one out of many, for such things proceed — whether spoken or through a look or a thousand other gestures — from hearts that love and are loved in return."

Viewing humanity as a society of friends elevates our way of thinking. It brings harmony and respect to matters human and divine. Love put into action by benevolent mercy brings goodness to everything. Since we find true friendship as we practice the virtues, what is contrary to virtue is contrary to friendship. Friendships that are sown in God and grow with God on our earthly sojourn will continue to reap rewards in our everlasting home.

God in his love has given us many wonderful gifts. We show our love as we embody his mercy and care for his gifts in practical ways. His great gift, which shows his faith and trust in us, is free will which places the earth in our hands. It is up to us to make things work in harmony with each other and the land. God is not the one who causes wars, inequality, or any of the other evils of our society. At times we would like to blame God for the ravages against humankind, but they are our fault. When God made the world, it was free of sin. He gave us hearts, brains, mouths and hands, and through them we choose daily to either respect or reject his world.

We cannot seek health and wholeness for ourselves or our earth apart from holiness. Holiness stands out as our primary quest. Wholeness and integration develop within holiness throughout our lives. We human beings are like a living symphony of love. Our melodies blend when our musical performances improve with practice and alterations. Atonal movements balance lightsome lyrics. Great crescendos appear with consonance and dissonance. Harmonies arise from discord, and silence is the pinnacle of smooth orchestration.

God and love are neither "nice" nor "sweet." Like the love songs of spring, the experience of God and love can be blissfully wonderful for a honeymoon length of time. A person with these blissful ideas may be living a fantasy if he or she experiences them indefinitely. God and his love are incomprehensible. We do not know what is going on or coming next. How easy it is to see God's reflections in the beauties of nature. Is it as easy to see him in corruption, calamity or confusion? C.S. Lewis wrote: "Holy places are dark places. It is life and strength, not knowledge and words, that we get in them. Holy wisdom is not clear and thin like water, but dark and thick like blood." We locate holiness by looking for God in our own darkness. Knowing ourselves in our darkness is beginning to know the truths about ourselves and acting on these truths. Authentic self-knowledge has its base in truth.

The more we find ourselves in Christ, the greater we will experience a true thirst for God. We have a spiritual and physical thirst for water. Jesus said: "I thirst," when he was on the cross, and implied much more than a physical need. At its deepest level Jesus' thirst was his desire for our love and our salvation. Jesus expressed his thirst to satisfy our thirst for the living water of which he has spoken previously. Without Jesus, we are like empty, dried-up water holes. He gives us living water which provides cleansing, refreshment, knowledge and life. We need his life-giving water every day and more so when our spiritual roots are dry and withered. Our failures and disappointments help us feel a little bit as Jesus did during the day and night before he was crucified. When the gentle rains fall into our lives after a long drought, we yearn for more. Water is true refreshment for those who drink deeply at the Eucharist and at prayer. When Jesus received the pain of insults, nails and a spear during his crucifixion, he responded with an outpouring of life-giving waters of forgiveness and mercy. We too can give these merciful cups of water to others in his name to lessen their physical and spiritual thirst.

The beauty of water is unending — a tree's reflection in a pond, rain in the woods, a field of flowers after a summer shower. What are they saying to us? A bird sits still and seemingly watches clouds drift by. The sun appears at dawn after the clouds of a night's storm move on. The first star of morning or the last star of evening peeks out from behind a lonely cloud. We experience a few moments of astounding wonder as we walk from here to there and ponder the splendorous forms of water around us. These moments can come anytime, anywhere, even in places we have rarely or never noticed before because beauty surrounds us. Leaves are more leafy, and everything is more brilliant and dazzling. How have we passed them by so often without noticing? We can find such a tremendous variety of life in the ocean's depth or a pail of water. A few drops of water can surprise us with a life-absorbing vision. A few small drops of water, of grace or of mercy, can lay the groundwork for new growth for the rest of our lives.

Water symbolizes grace from the Holy Spirit. It is from water that all things are made new. Rain nurtures vegetation and animal life. It falls from the heavens and flows in rivers, streams, creeks and irrigation. It remains in puddles, ponds and oceans and sustains palm trees, prairie life and plants of all kinds. Nothing created can live very long without water. So too can we not live without the waters of grace.

The Holy Spirit, of one essence with, yet proceeding from, the Father and the Son, sends graces to people as they need them. Each person's graces are different in manner and form. Yet the Holy Spirit is one and the same, like the rain. The Spirit flows from the Father and the Son in unparalleled mystery. As gifts of rest in labor, refreshment in heat, solace in tears and strength in temptation these graces from the Holy Spirit are the sustainers of life. On the physical plane we illustrate how the Holy Spirit gives life and cleanses, as we watch life unfold after a spring rain clears the air. The workings of the Spirit are well symbolized by the rain as it washes, refreshes and brings new life to the dry earth.

With the grace of the Holy Spirit, we can look all around us with the eyes of our soul and even the ugly becomes beautiful. Even though the world remains an enigma, grace is beauteous and with it we can remove the forces that spoil our earth. Human furies and their consequences scar the face of mother earth. Yes, there is evil, hardships and twisted and tragic lives. Yet, deep inside there is good. We locate the good, look at it, and treasure it, rather than that which is so apparent. We go beyond our puddles of petty, immediate self-preoccupations and locate the river which flows to eternity. It forms from the spring of the sanctity of life. As gift, it flows by all of us, always moving to God who is more vast than the sea and sky and whose mercy endures forever.

As Grateful Stewards

Our land is sacred as mother earth and home to us. A continuous movement of people throughout time and history have trod upon this land. While the soil grows food for life and soaks in the blood of the dying, homes are built on the land and the dead are buried in it. The earth receives the sweat of our labors and the tears of our sorrows and joys.

Our journey on this land is brief. A life is like one drop of water in a vast ocean of time. This everlasting sea extends from past to future and touches the lives of all human beings. Its shoreline can be life-giving if we live in sound moral and spiritual climates, because such climates pull the extremes in the world together: the rich and poor, the educated and illiterate, the occidental and oriental, the fortunate and unfortunate. The mysteries of life are always within and around this sea, passing through the intellect and probing into new ways of thinking. Although we gaze in awe at what we do not understand, we still know that the world must be repaired and renewed, and that we are its menders and furbishers. During our brief time here, and through the grace of God, we are the minor creators and artists of the earth.

The environment reveals much beauty as we gently probe its cracks, crannies and crevices. So do people, if we are gentle with them. When we become wise in the use of the resources of creation and sensitive to the needs of living things, we need not place technical knowledge on a pedestal. Technology is at its best when we use it to serve legitimate human needs. Technology that serves the human family is welcome; it is unwelcome when individuals become servants to technology. Since a reverent vision of life lets us see beyond the immediacies of today to the deeper realities of the future, the beauties of nature bring us into solidarity with the human condition. Everyone in the human family is vulnerable to fragmentation in the sufferings of being human and in the havoc that nature can wreak. Hurricanes, earthquakes, floods, freezing winters and scorching summers can cause great trauma, loss and despair. On the other hand, these disasters can bring people together in neighborhoods, cities and rural areas. Aid may come from neighbors people never knew they had or even from the other side of the world. Heroic rescue efforts in natural disasters show there is no life unworthy of life. If the effects of trauma cannot be cured, Good Samaritans continue to give care because it is in and through our shared humanity that God works.

Goodness and beauty unfold in the seasons of time and the seasons of our lives. Recognizable periods of growth contrast with periods which seem to be dormant. Without the death and decay of winter, the earth could not replenish itself for spring. The changes on the earth parallel changes in our own lives. From barren to bounteous, the seasons of creation around us contrast and complement the changes of seasons within us.

Throughout our lives, each of us reflects the image of God in different ways. During a single day, we may fluctuate between reflections of his benevolence and his wrath. As God's work of creation manifests his wisdom, so do we show our wisdom through the decisions we make or fail to make, all of which support or depose God's call to love. Like the changing seasons, the certainties of our present time can open us to new life through the risks of love. Just as winter's decaying leaves enrich the soil that gives life to the new plants of spring, we walk through the dark death of an ending to find the light's dawning of a new beginning. Each new beginning challenges us to care for others. Growth of wisdom that comes with each beginning makes us realize that caring love is tough and tender. Good care does not deplete the emotions of the giver or stifle the efforts of the receiver. We know we should not mire ourselves in caring for others to the point of being destructive to ourselves. Caring love sustains the giver's and receiver's balance by letting them maintain a grip on reality. Yes, as caring people we are moved by the components of whatever evokes our care, but are not swept away by them. Any plant, animal or human being grows better when it is not beset by wild emotions or radical actions from those who care for it.

Good stewardship is a distinct call of authentic Christians, and a sound mark of Carmelites on the mountain. To care for the inexhaustible gifts of God's creation is a serious responsibility Carmelites take to heart. As pilgrims in Carmel, we find much joy in the textures, scents, shapes, sounds and sights of the earth. We also find joy in being caretakers of God's gifts and consider this a sacred privilege. We find God and his mastery in all aspects of nature especially when we discover that scientific explanations can go only so far. Gerard Manley Hopkins wrote a plea to preserve nature: "What would the world be once bereft of wet and wildness? Let them be left, O let them be left, wildness and wet: Long live the weeds and the wilderness yet."

If we live close to the rhythm of the earth we become more sensitive to its mysteries: The heady scents of spring penetrating, the damp of earth ascending, the splendor of summer's sun rising, the color of autumn's leaves descending, the silent snow of winter falling. All seems quiet as nature moves through enchanting cycles. How out of step our throw-away habits are with the ebb and flow of nature. However, if we wish to preserve that natural ebb and flow, we must have cause to do such things like thinking twice the next time we use something once and toss it in the trash. Second thoughts encourage us to sort and recycle trash and purchase long-lasting items. Day by day our efforts may seem minor, yet, if we can envision them across a lifetime, we will have made a sound contribution to the wet and the wild. If we do not care for people and things in our immediate environment in the short run, things such as social justice and preservation mean little in the long run. As we join our efforts with others, our small efforts become sound gains. Positive things we do together shape and strengthen the communities in which we live. To realize this, we have only to reflect upon the barn raisings, quilting parties and harvests of country life. These and other community activities affirm the connection of neighbors with each other and with the seasons of creation. Stewardship is doing what we can to restore the goodness of the earth and its people wherever we live.

To gaze from Mount Carmel is to understand the sacred responsibility to reverence and care for the earth by becoming prudent in the use of its resources. In order to live in harmony with the land and promote responsible stewardship, Carmelite pilgrims must live a lifestyle that witnesses to a concern for the earth and all creation. Those of us who view life from the mountain can join organizations that try to heal the wounds that have been inflicted upon our land; or we can provide others with educational materials that promote good use of the land and its resources. We can keep outdoor areas, from national parks to city streets, clean and tidy, and if we use the land for financial profit we can do so in an accountable manner. By keeping in mind the need to maintain the good quality of soil, air and water, and the balance of animal and plant life, all who seek God share in keeping the earth and its atmosphere healthy. There are a countless number of good ways to participate in the well-being of our land. The view from the slopes of Mount Carmel reminds us that all land is holy.

Concern for people and concern for the environment walk hand in hand. Destruction of the resources that future generations will need contradicts what it means to protect and sustain life around us. Environmental concerns are actually universal; a regional problem affects us all. Rampant consumerism by the industrialized world increases poverty in the third world. Air pollutants and water that contain chemical spills cross boundaries between countries. Oil spills kill animals in the sea and on the shore. Acid rain permeates places that did not create it. New landfills adversely affect rivers and lakes. Depletion of the ozone layer and reduction of forests have global consequences.

Gradually we can increase our responsibility toward our earth and its people through preservation, protection, information and practical application. Our wisdom and insights can noticeably reduce strains and stresses on our natural resources, as we develop a sound appreciation of the goodness of God's creation. When we discover greater goodness, we widen our foundation in accountability to the environment. Compassion for people and all creation increases the balance between humanity and the natural world. As long as we preserve the beauty of nature and assist in its productivity, we will find unique rewards in the fruits of our harvest.

Family farms of moderate size were regarded as the cornerstone of American agriculture. The work was hard and the hours long. While sustaining a wholesome lifestyle, the family worked together through cooperation and shared responsibilities. The hardships and rewards bonded members of the family to each other, and gave strength to the family as a unit. Today, however, family farms have declined by the thousands and have been replaced by large corporate farms. Corporate farms, while making it possible to feed the world's burgeoning population with the limited amount of arable land available, regrettably rate profit above husbandry. As a result, the transition to corporate agriculture has depleted the quality of air, soil and water and caused many rural communities and small towns to collapse.

We show respect for the land when we use appropriate technology in our living and working areas. This includes the protection of endangered species and natural environments. The effects of inappropriate land use and soil erosion are felt by everyone. Although urban concerns have more visibility in the news media than rural matters, it is said that each depression is farm led and farm fed. Top soil is part of the skin that sustains life on our planet and, although we are losing this skin, how often do we talk about the problems of agriculture? The difficulties of farmers eventually become the difficulties of businesses and community structures. One solution that would benefit rural America, unfortunately unlikely given the present structure of our economy, would be a decrease of large corporate farm interests. Rural community farms and local businesses promote individual respect for the land in several ways. Crops can grow in harmony with the limits of the soil. Shopping locally saves money and time. Merchants can support family farms and supply what they need. Community members can own or shop at businesses and thus promote sustainable community development. Sound relations between individuals and businesses begin with moral solidarity that encourages equitable development and discourages destructive over-development. Businesses can encourage land owners to practice socially responsible and environmentally sound land use, because how owners treat their land determines how they value it. A serious thought upon which to reflect is that rural communities and small towns convey a sense of place and identity that is unfamiliar in industrial, mobile urban areas.

With God's help we can maintain a sense of the sacred regarding our land, lakes, forests, pastures, cities, skies, the water we drink, the air we breathe and the people we meet. By manifesting the strength of our faith through the strength of our responsibility for creation, our participation in a common effort to right what is wrong helps reshape man-made systems to better serve the earth. People with a sound theological foundation develop an ethically and morally strong communion and community by working together toward sustainable agriculture, good health, and fair economics.

If we review our past and reflect on whether our behavior has sustained the earth and honored its people, we are more mindful of our personal response to our surroundings. A personal response would be empty without the reality of God in our lives. An authentic environmental consciousness must be spiritually awake, alert and informed. Prayers of the season join God with the earth. We may offer planting and harvest prayers for a seed in a planter, a small garden or large field. Travel or relocation prayers bless a vacation, long journey or move from apartment to house, city to country or state to state. Short prayers weave the sacred into struggles, joys, daily routine and lifetime changes. A personal relationship with God is the baseline of an authentic environmental consciousness.

If we are serious about conservation, we should participate in related activities without fanfare or flourish so that it becomes ingrained in our being and unobtrusively influences each aspect of our lives. Newspapers, glass, plastic and metal we no longer need are directed to recycling centers. This reduces industrial pollution and waste in landfills. It also saves trees in the forest and sand on the beach. We carry home items from the grocery stores in canvas bags. We buy food items in recycled containers and in bulk which reduces packing materials. We use padded mailing envelopes, aluminum foil, and gift wrap more than once. We consider the value of solar panels. We plant a tree to honor a loved one and thereby give a gift of lasting beauty. Ways of restoring and maintaining a clean and balanced environment are plentiful and, hopefully, many more are yet to be discovered. Through our efforts, we can experience anew the natural, awesome beauty of falling rain, chirping birds, blowing wind and rumbling thunder. Physical contact with the soil and water brings people back to their roots. A trip to the beach or mountains, with sunlight and fresh air, are forces that dilute man-made stresses and restore nature with human existence. Growing plants, smelling flowers or going barefoot on the grass brings a serendipity of delight to a dreary day. Indeed, the gifts of Mount Carmel refine or create innovative ways of perceiving the beauties of the earth.

To be true conservationists, we must question whether the companies with which we do business are ecologically responsible. What do they use for packaging and how is their merchandise shipped? Do they have employee service projects in the community to clean up the beach, build houses, reduce toxic waste, plant seedlings or participate in other related activities? Social responsibility for the environment should be a part of a corporate charter. High profit is not the ultimate measure of the effectiveness of a business. The purpose of a business is to provide a needed service or goods and maintain ecological accountability. A reasonable profit is one that makes it possible to continue to provide services or goods and provide a decent living wage for the employees and their dependents. Conservation is the responsibility of corporations as well as individuals.

If change is needed in a corporation, it must begin with internal operations. Do the raw materials and processes of product fabrication deplete or destroy natural resources? Because every product ultimately has an environmental impact, waste management, use of chemicals and many other aspects of a corporate business affect the environment. Workers in a factory indirectly connect with the animals, forests, sky, rivers and other people. Choices made by people in any business influence the destiny of life on planet earth.

Collaboration and commitment from people in all walks of life, scientific research and technological innovation must coexist with sound religious and moral codes in order to meet the environmental challenge. Faith is not a substitute for facts. Faith based on gospel teachings guides facts to practical applications. Reverence for creation begins with reverence for God. It develops through an ecologically responsible morality and provides applications through human reasoning and scientific endeavors. All combine to form a reverent respect for the great gift of life.

Love urges our efforts so that all people may share in the bounty of the earth. A blend of restraint and innovation combine with the virtues of prudence, humility and temperance to become indispensable elements for equal rights. As long as we forgive ourselves and others we have the potential to become co-creators of new beginnings. By relying on faith, hope and love to sustain us, we can evolve from consumers of the earth to stewards of the earth. The fruits of the earth are meant to sustain the whole human family within a just economic system. Ecological responsibility will reach its peak when humanity shows compassion and mercy to its weakest members. A decent environment supports a decent life for all people who inhabit it. Therefore, we cannot preserve wildlife, yet callously ignore our elderly or others in the marginal regions of life. There is a spiritual connection in all creation. Care for creation is at its best when it stems from faith in God and concern for our neighbors.

The Carmelite Order began in the Holy Land on Mount Carmel. Carmelite pilgrims of the mountain have a special call to respect and protect the earth. Often God and his love are met in the mountains, deserts, waterways, gentle breezes and, most frequently, in the tender love of quiet whispers. Such has been the way of Carmel through the ages. As Carmelites we are greatly blessed since the beauties of nature take us to where creation was conceived. As men and women of the mountain, we follow the call to be reverent toward, and responsible for, the environment wherever we live. God's gifts of plants, animals, water, land, home, work and Church must have a significant place in the Carmelite's prayer and care, making us unique stewards of God's earth. The diversity of life on the earth continually reveals the glory of God. A sacramental awareness of stewardship is Carmel's sacred trust as each member recaptures the awesome wonder of the fullness of life. Long, loving looks at what is in and around the pilgrims of Carmel help join creation and creator together in loving, silent songs of praise. From the smallest molecule to the vastness of space, all creation is a gift in and with Christ.

With his great love, and God's grace, John of the Cross rose to the heights of mystical prayer. He experienced total union with Christ who is forever united with God. After he passed through the prayer of transforming union John penned the following: "Mine are the heavens and mine is the earth. Mine are the nations, the just are mine, and mine the sinners. The angels are mine, and the Mother of God and all things are mine, and God himself is mine and for me, because Christ is mine and all for me."

8

On the Mountain

That which I am I offer to you, O Lord, without looking to any quality of your being, but only to the fact that you are as you are. This and nothing more.   *John of the Cross*

Ever before us, Mount Carmel symbolizes the challenge of a climb. As Carmelites we dare not tarry near the base of that mountain. We pack our knapsack for a laborious adventure and take the first steps into a lifelong journey.

At times we will travel in a group, and in the beginning it is rather large. We give our fellow travelers encouragement and support, pulling some up, pushing others ahead, or assisting those who walk by our sides. Later on, we travel at our own pace. Far into the journey there will be distances we travel alone, along rocky trails or up craggy cliffs. Although our journey to God will have solitary times we will never forget our fellow pilgrims, as we keep them in our hearts. Our lone search for God is fortified by a burning desire to bring others to God. As we walk we rediscover the wisdom of relying on God, the importance of prayer, the necessity of working diligently and resting as we need it. Mount Carmel never ceases to challenge us. The radix of the mountain is deep in the primordial needs of the earth and the people who inhabit it. The earth keeps our feet on the ground. The peak of the mountain pierces the sky and directs us to the Triune God. The sky keeps our eyes on Christ. Mount Carmel and her mountaineers connect earth and heaven, time and eternity, secular and sacred, mortality and immortality, creation and Christ. As Carmelite hikers on the mountainside, we experience hardships in prayer, yet remain enthralled by its supernatural essence. Prayer is the heartbeat of the soul, the sustenance of life, and the source of energy for movement on our uphill journey.

Spiritual wisdom is passed along by word of mouth on the mountain. Spiritual growth in the mountain wilderness is very different from what we find in classrooms of theology or seminars on religious topics. The hands of mountain-climbing Carmelites are rubbed raw from rocky holds and knees are deeply scarred from slides and falls. On dark days, musings fill our minds with gloom-drenched ideations: We made the climb but fell to where we started so long ago. We have lived a lifetime and have not grown a spiritual inch. We slipped to the foothills of the mountain so often we might as well chuck it. In time, the light of wisdom breaks up our gloomy thoughts. We realize that our faults and bad habits can trip us up, but as we work on them they can aid us on our journey. Tough love and naked trust maintain our hold on the steadfast ropes of faith and hope and keep our spiritual identity rugged and steadfast. Wisdom helps us to see through our mind-numbing times of gloom, as it adds compassion to our basic goodness and conversion to our weaknesses.

Since Carmel's beauty lies in continual conversion and compassion, we must increase our respect for the strengths and weaknesses in our fellow travelers as we acknowledge and work with that which is in ourselves. It is not uncommon that attributes which we do not care for in others are often those we cannot face in ourselves. If our call to compassion is to ring true, it is accompanied by a call to conversion. Compassion provides changes that are lifesaving, while conversion is an inner change of heart and mind. We can extend compassion and conversion to others in a way that does not hurt, patronize, condescend or attack. While compassion without conversion lacks spiritual substance, conversion without compassion is weak. However, combine them equally together and they open us to who people are, rather than what we need them to be.

Wisdom in compassion and conversion helps us to be more patient with ourselves and others who are close to us. It is so easy to extend compassion to strangers, because we never know them well enough to feel the sharp edges of their personalities. How much harder it is to be compassionate toward family and others we know well. Wisdom can teach us to like those we love while realizing we have sharp edges too.

Wisdom values substance above image, character and integrity above clever actions and popular linguistics, purity of heart above secret agendas, decency over corruption and forthrightness over subtle cynicism. For that reason, wisdom gives us the strength to frequently check how much time we give to the various forms of media and how they influence us. By regulating and limiting our media involvement, we will not numb our spiritual sensitivities or retard contact with our deeper levels of being. It is known that we absorb media violence and its other characteristics, including inspirational programs, through our senses. Then they pass through us and reappear in various ways through our behavior and attitudes.

The overall goodness we convey increases the unity and the love among the people of God. Goodness bonds with wisdom and aids us in discerning how to keep the best of the past and the best of the present. The graces from this type of discernment suggest to us what we should do with what we have. By seeking and finding God in ourselves and in each other, we discover the completeness of his forgiveness and love and they become our way of enlightenment. Ultimately, the degree to which we forgive and love will be the degree to which we see the face of God.

In order to continue our search for God with renewed vigor and reawaken the strange and mysterious elements in the depths of our souls, we are ever vigilant in prayer. We pray in unity with others and prayer takes us apart. No longer is prayer an expression of what we do each day, it becomes the basic substance of who we are. Like a bubbling spring from which our service and dedication flow, prayer is the constant force which moves us forward. How easily we can fall behind or even fall into the valley of the shadow if we discontinue the flow of daily prayer, even for a short time. The higher our climb, the more intense our need for prayer and the more immense our need for God becomes. Prayer manifests the reality of our own incompleteness and bonds us to the ever-lasting totality of God.

As Carmelites climbing the mountain we are at our best when we are not aware we are making the climb. We can illustrate this by the following story: One day an ant watched a centipede walk. The ant was fascinated by the way the centipede moved. The ant asked the centipede: "How do you keep all your legs moving without getting them all tangled up?" The centipede stopped to think about it and never moved again. Like the centipede, we are at our prime when we are not cognizant of the rigors of the journey. If we examine our lives with microscopic detail, it may well lead to the torments of perfectionism or the termination of motion. The higher our ascent the less we need to seriously analyze what is happening in our lives or in those around us. Carmel's essence should take us eons beyond morbid preoccupation with and vocal-ization about self or others. A gift of the mountain is a judicious acuity regarding the difference between sound introspection and destructive analysis about self, and when to speak and when to remain silent about others. Beauteous discoveries await, as the spirit of Carmel entices us to find our center in Christ. As long as we keep our eyes on our true center, we can strive forward with an uncluttered heart and seek God with a receptive mind.

Mary and Elijah point out the way to us. Mary was the first pioneer to blaze our trail. Throughout her life she lived by faith and trust and deeply pondered all that happened to her. She is the unparalleled model for living a life of pure faith. We look to Mary and understand how to listen and answer God, and the way to contemplate his message. She shows us how to be open to God through prayer, to ourselves through self-knowledge, and to others through selfless service. Elijah's spirit echoes through the mountain peaks, as he teaches us how to live in the presence of God and be attentive to the changes of our time. He challenges us to confront the misuse of religious and secular authority and to pay attention to those whom society would like to forget.

As we move higher on the mountain, our focus on God becomes clearer. We transform slowly as we cease seeing God solely as a benevolent, benign being, someone who heals us, gives us material or spiritual goodies, or gets us out of trouble. This is loving the gifts of God, not God himself. To see God as someone who sweetly satisfies our desires is to be spiritually myopic. So, we must strive to love God not because it is sweet to love him, but because it is right and just to love him.

God is ultimate love for whom we are grateful and to whom we channel all aspects of our lives. As Carmelites we witness to the grandeur of God and the primacy of prayer in our lives by the way we attend to the details in our days. As prayer takes the first priority in our days, we learn to love the mystery of God's love in adoration, celebration, sorrow, communion and companionship. Always, always we aspire to a deeper seeking after his love. Prayer enfolds us in God's love and unfolds in our service to others. To infuse his love into the world is a most honorable and never ending vocation. The world is more in need of prayers from people filled with God's love than of works from mediocre Christians. Those who sincerely pray perpetually encounter God's love, for the depths of God can never be fully fathomed.

As time goes by on our mountain climb, we can see clearly our own aspirations and longings within the vision of God's love. As his vision comes to pass, we should reflect upon our desires humbly, gently and honestly. As we reach out to what God teaches us through his love in our lives, we grasp what adds and detracts from our own ability to love. Although our unique experiences in love shape and form us individually and collectively, we real-ize that God's everlasting love is what draws us to, and keeps us moving in, Carmel.

Mount Carmel is a symbol for our ascent, our interior adventure, our spiritual journey in the frontiers of our soul. Our mountain climb will not be reported in the newspapers or maga-zines. Nor will it be a topic for a television series or a movie. Even if we are beset by avalanches, serious falls, abandonment, starva-tion or savage beasts, few people will take notice of our wilderness adventure and there will be no breaking news coverage or special reports. For us, only the light of faith directs and supports us as we hunger, thirst, lose our way or fall from grace. At the beginning, the journey seems endless as we waiver to and fro and vacillate from side to side. Nonetheless, the pinnacle of transforming union spurs us on. Many things will happen that we do not understand, but the higher we climb, the less we need to understand. Wisdom from the Holy Spirit swirls around us in quiet whispers: Do not be afraid. Let God take the lead, and accept what comes along with love.

Heartbeat

A scattering of spiritual graves are notable along the edges of the wide and smooth road which marks the beginning of the spiritual journey. Corpses under the tombstones have living com-panions with like minds who breeze past their markers with nary a glance. These tenderfoots have stars in their eyes as they walk along in a magical mist. However, if they continue their spiritual fantasy, they too will soon be under the sod and the dew, because they are quite taken by the sweets they find in prayer. To them, prayer is like a cuddly, soft blanket. So it is easy to love and pray when the heart feels like warm sunshine. Aged hikers may caution these novices that the test for prayer comes when prayer is like a cold rain in an empty heart. However, these tenderfoots often persist in entertaining sweet and lovely thoughts, and so do not persevere on the trail to God. Thankfully, most of us pass through the meadows of this sugarplum stage of spirituality. After this stage prayer may still be a delectable experience now and then but, more often it is hard. Nevertheless, like an old redwood tree, it is strong and sturdy. Redwood tree prayer cuts through feathery fluff. Mystical magic, holy superstitions or winsome inclinations soon wither and blow away in the wind, like dead leaves. Our bare trees of prayer stand firm when we see God as he is, not as we want him to be.

Let us look at an example. We may pray for an end to verbal abuse, not simply by asking God to intervene, but by suggesting to him the many ways he can change others. When things do not happen the way we want, we can instead listen and wait. At the point where we truly listen, he quietly shows us his ways. His ways can then become the ways by which we contend with the abuse. However, because God's ways are not what we expected, instead of watching others change we will find change in ourselves and take good action. Indeed, God answers our prayers through our transformation. So, we need not think about what God should do within others and respond to what he is doing in ourselves.

The heart and life's blood of Carmel is Christocentric prayer. After we settle into the school of Carmel, prayer becomes the most natural element in our day. Carmel offers no sophisticated studies in specialized areas of prayer. Nor does it offer detailed analysis, synthesis or dissection of prayer. No excessive emphasis is placed on the theological or philosophical aspects of prayer. Carmel does not mandate any particular method or technique of prayer. Even though techniques are helpful to a point, they are far from the main ingredients for sound and lasting prayer in our mystical school. Note that nothing in Scripture describes how to meditate or contemplate, and methods may not even impress God.

Carmel offers sound assistance and a deeper understanding of prayer as a communion of love with God. We only become specialists in prayer when we live the gospel without reserve. New discoveries or inventions in prayer are minor trails in the mountain school of Carmel. Instead, the Carmelite school is like a rough guide, which is close to the wild, with a strong instinct for spiritual survival. The few, tattered pages of our Carmelite guide emphasize intimacy within prayer, the heartbeat of our spiritual lives.

Prayer is the preeminent and predominant way to pursue God and draw nearer to him. In this way, the pursuit of knowledge is not an end in itself, but a means to greater understanding of the truths of God. However, experiences resulting from extraordinary prayer or mystical phenomena are unnecessary for advancement in the Carmelite school of spirituality. As a matter of fact, Carmelites matriculate quite well without them. Since extraordinary spiritual events are a sub-specialty in the Carmelite study of prayer, major courses of study are aimed rather at the discovery of God.

The Carmelite school teaches the eminent need for, and appreciation of, authentic prayer in our lives. Commitment to prayer in Carmel is basically realized in quiet, solitary prayer. If God is to be quietly behind everything we think, say and do, our credibility as praying Carmelites depends on our faithful living of the whole gospel. Our good actions rely on support from our solitary prayer. This quiet prayer can be as simple as an affectionate sigh or a loving gaze at the heart of God. Herein lies the still point of our turning world. Prayer is not a part of the framework of our lives; rather it is the center of the foundation on which we build our lives. The essence of prayer lies in what we give rather than what we receive, and how we love rather than what we think. Indeed, some people can pray intensely without realizing they are praying while others can place high value on their prayer, and their prayer is actually very weak. A grace from prayer teaches us that we live to the extent by which we give action to our good intentions. Faithful adherence to daily, quiet prayer is manifest in a prayerful presence inherent in who we are and what we do outside of prayer.

Carmelite students of prayer can be compared to sleepy

cows under trees in a pasture. These cows settle down and chew their cud peacefully and continuously, as they savor the flavor and relish the present moment. The "prayer of contented cows" seems superbly Carmelite. It imparts tranquillity, captivation and patient integration, which is not a bad way to eat or pray. Since the prayer of contentment gives us time in silence to pause, we can turn things over, repeat them slowly and cradle new insights. Quietly they sway to and fro in our interior milieu, as we ruminate on them, chew them again and assimilate them into our being. Blessed be he or she who ruminates well upon the words of our Lord Jesus. His sacred teachings and Eucharistic food must be chewed again and again. When we do this over and over and experience conversional nourishment in mind, heart and soul, this holy food, fully consumed, drops down into the inmost places of our hearts. Once there it spreads to all our members and helps us conduct ourselves more in the manner of Jesus.

As student hikers on Mount Carmel, we must aspire to be professionals in prayer. This lofty and awesome call requires life-long learning, but such expertise merits an undergraduate degree in a visible aspect of God's love: humility. Humility keeps us in proper alignment with God and with ourselves. Through humility we let ourselves be loved by God, while realizing our true worth as unique and valued people of God. At the same time, humility puts the damper on the need to control, complain, make excuses, be calculating or tell stories that make us look or feel good. Humility reminds us what to do if we have a strong urge to boast about how often we pray, or the greatness of our prayers or ministries. We only need to place our feet in a pail of water. When we remove our feet, the hole that remains will give us the correct measure of our importance.

> The tumult and the shouting dies,
>   The captains and the kings depart;
> Still stands Thine ancient sacrifice,

A humble and a contrite heart:
Lord God of Hosts, be with us yet,
Lest we forget, lest we forget.
Rudyard Kipling

Prayer for the Carmelite is often not a great or rewarding spiritual, emotional or mental experience. Therefore, rare are the fancy frills or spiritual thrills. Since our fundamental reason for praying should be more preparatory than pragmatic, we can ready ourselves for whatever God sends our way. Spiritual insights will come more readily when we quiet the imagination and control the senses. We refine and elevate our personal and communal prayer when they are no longer dependent on stimulation from the senses or imagination such as those provided by cultural influences. While cultural expressions of prayer are good to a certain degree because they keep us in touch with our heritage and may be stimulating or consoling, there is a vast spiritual area of prayer beyond cultural expression. We realize we are more than cultural Christians since the values and practices of a culture change and it is subject to folklore and superstition. God is beyond cultures and does not change. We must bypass our known regional areas and fly with wings of grace into the universal mystery of God's space before we can truly experience his unique omnipresence.

The time will come when we may no longer receive a sensory or emotional shot in the arm from personal or communal prayer. This should not be of concern since it may be an introduction to a higher form of prayer. It is wise to remember that the spiritual journey does not depend on the emotions of the moment, but rather on the perseverance of a lifetime. Divine wisdom helps us to remember that, when our prayer feels like absolute zero, we can offer it as a gift of pure love.

So sometimes our prayer will be very flat and dry. We have nothing to show for it, or so we think. While we are doing something quite routine, a spiritual insight may creep into our thoughts, seemingly to have come from nowhere. However, deep inside we know its origin. We understand the purpose of prayer: to get nearer to God. When our maps are designed by him, movement in the right direction happens in moments of prayer, or at the oddest moments outside of prayer.

Once upon a time a Carmelite novice wanted to learn how to pray. She spoke of this desire to her novice director who replied: "You do not even know how to close a door. Practice closing a door with reverent attention and you may find it opens to infinity." The novice director shows us we need to be spiritually awake and pay reverent attention to whatever we are doing. Wherever we are, self-discipline and grace keep us in the presence of God. Little spiritual fruits surprise us as we find them in anything we do with love, even closing a door. Sometimes they are bright and easy to locate, very much like red cherry tomatoes or ripe strawberries. At other times they camouflage or hide among prickly thorns or sticky bushes. Spiritual fruits bud from our prayerful presence and, with sharp spiritual vision as they are easy to miss, we can find them anytime and anywhere. As small lights reflecting the everlasting light of faith, they can become more precious than flickering lights reflecting the momentary happiness of spectacular events.

Carmelite prayer reaches into the innermost areas of our being and out to the vastness of the universe. Prayer is neither time spent avoiding the external responsibilities of life, nor time spent dreaming up mystical musings of our own making. Instead, the roots of prayer connect our hearts with the heart of life on earth. To fully recognize this is to be quite sensitive to the graces of silent prayer. The hidden, quiet energy which keeps all things moving in the right direction comes from prayer. It is a vast source of unseen, spiritual strength and a daily recognition of the eternal dimensions of life. Quiet prayer calms us down so we become more teachable, while freeing us up to be more attentive to the delicate signs of God's presence that are within and around us.

Prayer is never an escape from life. More accurately it is

a means by which we enter more deeply into life. When we reflectively read Scripture and assimilate it within the traditions of the Church we can then constructively think about practical applications and implement them in our internal and external life situations. Implementation is the life's blood that circulates from the heart of Carmel which is, forever and ever, prayer. The more we live the gospel the more prayer becomes the most central aspect of our being. Our practice of work a day prayer develops from our will, rather than from our emotions. The Carmelite trail will never be a pain-free journey because even in prayer there is pain. We pray when there are many other things we would rather do and when our lights to reform seem too bright to follow. However, when we look backward we see how pain shatters and strengthens prayer. Carmel gives us a vision of prayer that reaches far beyond our current inclinations or the limits of this world. We experience the call to Carmel at the center of our souls. Carmel's call to prayer is more powerful than any contradictory force inside or around us.

Suffering will be our lot in one way or another while we live on earth where everyone has the gift of free will. While some use free will wisely, others do not and they need our prayers of mercy for their decaying souls, and the souls they harm. Many tear-drenched prayers are offered for loved ones in turmoil. Paul's words are like a stout walking stick in this vale of tears: "All things work to the good for those who love God." This confirmation of God's wish to bring good out of anything is indeed a sturdy support. Yes, Carmel is a land of contrasts encompassing enchanting spiritual beauties and wretched temporal realities. In all of this, we can take heart that God is always with us, especially when he seems most absent, or when we encounter discouragement in prayer or abandonment by others.

The grief of the world is enough to keep our eyes cast down forever but we gaze ahead steadfast in hope. Hope reminds us that God is creator and redeemer and faithful in judgment and grace. In a world with so many complex and unanswered questions hope enables us to settle down, step forward with complete trust in God and continue on. As the captain said to the sailor, "We must trust in God, but row for shore."

In Carmel, prayer is the primary means of evangelization. Day in and day out, our orisons keep us touching the sacred and channeling it into the godless facets of life. When we tenderly place those who need, hurt or despair in the heart of Christ, we give visible witness to the sacred by living out our prayer. The energy created by prayer helps us to alter the godless aspects of society as we keep on living simply, remaining faithful to our duties, giving service and building loving relationships. Yes, the more we pray, the more we realize how all life is interconnected and interdependent.

As Carmelites we must be faithful and vigilant in prayer as ways to pray come and go and may be beneficial for a short time or a lifetime. The seasons of our prayer resemble the actions of nature on a stream. The water flows by us in the summer's sunlight, sparkling and shining. In the fall, leaves, twigs and other debris float by and cold, harsh winds cause the water to ruffle or foam. Winter's water is unseen, covered from view by thick, white ice. When spring comes round again, the clear water almost dances past bright, green foliage. Just as the water changes with the seasons, so should we be open to all that comes and goes, taking our prayer life as it comes. Even if it seems cold as ice, we know that in time, the prayer of winter will pass. Indeed, our prayer will, of necessity, spend periods in dark deep winters before it can flow in the bright joy of springtime.

Changes in the character of our active prayer are not unlike the changes in a stream exposed to the elements of nature. Reflective prayer takes place through grace and the work of our minds. Close to the surface of our lives, this prayer is constantly exposed to elements from our ever-changing feelings and desires. Because, as Carmelites, we are not confined to a particular method of prayer, we can let go of a certain type of prayer if it becomes overly burdensome or overly satisfying. A few different approaches to prayer also prevent a fixation with or glorification of a particular type of prayer. Although it is comfortable to remain in a self-satisfying type of prayer with hope for its desired effect, it does resemble a languid wait to catch fish in a well-known lake on a warm summer's day. However, Carmel is not a pleasurable dude ranch or leisure fun-filled resort. It is often more fitting for us to experience the bewilderment and discomfort of a new form of prayer because this less-traveled road may reveal mysteries of God previously unknown. The only way for us to find these new mysteries is to forge ahead. The true peace and beauty of prayer is found underneath the temperamental darks and lights of the seasons in our lives. Below the surface, we delight in a more open receptivity to God. In the depths of our souls we bond with him by quiet heart to heart communion and transparent attentiveness to his love which are far beyond the workings of our minds.

Carmelite prayer may cause the soul to cry out as its mysterious polarities pull it in different directions. We are grounded in God but, at the same time, seek him. He is elusive, yet knows us better than we know ourselves. As we lie prostrate from the burning wounds of self-knowledge, we cry out to God in the only words that make any sense: "Lord be merciful to me, a sinner." Since humility is the fuel of prayer, it keeps us from inappropriate pride in our spiritual accomplishments, or morbid thoughts about our sins and failures. Viable faith exposes us to the vastness of God's wisdom, yet keeps us humble about our own. There is much about adoration, contrition, thanksgiving and supplication that is beyond what we feel or understand. Knowing by unknowing, we blindly fly on wings of faith into the unknown. We set our sights on a God whom we cannot see, but who loves us infinitely.

Contemplative Wooded Slopes

God knows the evils within us and our society, but prayer stokes the fires of his mercy. People who live in the world and sincerely pray for it are needed more than ever. Those who acknowledge the contemplative dimension in the world see a deep interconnectedness beneath the inequitable and troubled surface of the world. Despite all the evil we see around us, we come to a certain point on the spiritual road, to a place of relative calm concerning the paradoxes and mysteries of life. Underlying everything is support in the reality that we are all a part of the body of Christ. The knowledge that his mystical body has been sustained by the flow of graces through the ages, sustains and calms us. We rest in faith because these graces will continue until the end of time. Faith enables us to endure. We recognize the quality of our faith by the way we live throughout the day, trying our best, standing firm and being ever-watchful. Although our prayer is basically solitary, it reaches to the ends of the earth and embraces it. From the silent places of the heart it comes, like water from a fountain that sprinkles our dry, troubled world with love. As God draws and moves our hearts to contemplative prayer on his terms, wanting things to happen may prevent it from happening. That is why, in the contemplative dimension of prayer we learn we love God best when we let him have his way. While we develop in prayer, we listen with care and our words are few. Contemplative prayer initiates an interior mobility through a freedom from self-concerns. We descend into unknown realms of beauty or move inadvertently and locate hidden crevices that reveal private demons. We are not distraught at our findings because God is with us as we compassionately move around our inner spiritual realm. We know we must first reach into our spiritual depths before we can authentically reach out to others. As we rest in our contemplative space, we may think we move, but it is God who moves us. As we provide care, it is beyond something the strong gives the weak. A contemplative demeanor makes us at ease with not knowing or having the answers. Often there is little need to give advice, offer explanations or solutions, or share joy or pain with many words. We harmonize with our inner findings as we are moved quietly in the dark. As Carmelites we dwell, silently, with the unusual and remarkable call to be a contemplative in the Church and in the world through fidelity to our way of life. Fidelity is the outward manifestation of the pristine, wordless beauty of the mystery we call contemplation.

Our spiritual depths reveal that the sacred is the center point of all life on earth. We prune our excesses and harvest our sacred treasures, as we move from banal curiosity to the everlasting wisdom of God. A contemplative mobility makes everything we do with love holy, as a disciplined watch keeps relative order and harmony in our internal and external lives. Love grows as it is nourished by the sweet solitude of our prayer. It is not so much the love of a project, movement or ministry in which we are involved, but genuine love of people. An outcome of deep prayer is primarily a greater love for people and secondarily a work or ministry that might benefit them. Our prayer is the first means by which we build up the sacredness of the world for it unites the mystical body of Christ, and thereby improves the quality of life in the human family. The splendor of contemplative prayer is evident in choices for life which in turn enhance the sanctity of all life.

The travels of a Carmelite contemplative may be compared with the movements of a Conestoga wagon. The wheels of this prairie schooner turn slowly as they move the wagon along the rugged trail west. Part of the rim of the wheel always touches the earth, which illustrates how prayer always connects with the daily realities of life. The spokes connect the outer rim to the center of the wheel. Spokes represent things in our lives which lead us to our center, God. God is like the hub of the wheel because he is the nucleus of our lives. The spokes give the wheel the firmness it needs in order to move. The activities of each day are as spokes by which we move toward God. As there does not seem to be much change in scenery as our covered wagon crosses the lone prairie, so it is on the Carmelite trail. We may not notice what is happening day by day, yet step by step, we travel far. After many years in Carmel we can look back and know the journey, despite all its hardships, was well worth the effort put forth.

Contemplative prayer moves in a spectrum from utmost, tender simplicity to total, transformational unity. It can be likened to the poverty of open hands which receive anything, while never closing over what they receive. Contemplative receptivity, however, should not be mistaken for inertia. Instead, it constitutes the most essential part of the movement of humanity toward God, ever mindful that the purpose of prayer is to know and love God better. As we step over the contemplative threshold, we come to know that contentment, like prayer, does not need to be pursued. Both come to us as we live our lives for the glory of God. A deeply prayerful person is a contented person, and contentment, as we understand, depends more on disposition than on circumstances. Likewise, contentment in prayer is not so much found in the good experiences we receive from prayer, as in discovering new ways of knowing and loving God.

Easy access to contemplation is very rare. A contemplative attentiveness to life, ever wakeful and alert, is a gift of grace. Contemplatives build up the Church primarily through prayer and, secondarily, through service for love of God and others. Within the contemplative ideal work is subordinate to prayer except, of course, in emergencies. While it is true that a good portion of our value as persons is found in the work we do, prayer purifies our motivations in work and keeps the various dimensions of our lives in a viable kinship. Indeed, we appreciate the necessity of a deep prayer life and the achievements of our labors. For a contemplative, work enriches life but does not become the reason for living because work is provisional, temporary and subject to change. Prayer is eternal.

Contemplative prayer may be likened to sun splashes on a shadowy path. The quiet lights of contemplation burn in silent determination to make this world a better place in which to live. By contributing to life through loving God and graciously caring for others directly or indirectly, contemplatives act locally and think globally. As we witness to the primacy of God in our lives, we pray his word may bear fruit in the hearts of others. Carmelites are most at home in the contemplative depths of life, as we descend through our own nothingness to delight in God within. We sense a spiritual freshness as words cease and we are mute, with a pure heart, in the immensity of God. No "self" is involved in true contemplative prayer. Utter receptivity to God suspends us in gentle repose and silent interior intimacy with him.

As contemplatives we intuitively know that others, mostly unknown to us, benefit as we move forward on our spiritual journey. Likewise, if we lose ground, or stop, other people lose. Contemplative attentiveness offers us a vision of who we might be and influences us toward improvement. The best effects of contemplative prayer are those which enable us to be better followers of Jesus Christ. Each day we renew our resolve to follow Jesus. Teresa tells us: "Christ does not force our wills. He will only take what we give him, but he will never give himself entirely to us until we give ourselves entirely to him."

Needless to say, we do not pray every day because we want to feel good or be holy. Prayer is not a psychological activity, social encounter or something to fill a mental void. Spiritual aerobics, mindless repetitions or exotic postures do not touch the heart of prayer. Our motivation to pray is sustained by the life of Jesus and rarely from our own romantic ideas. Contemplative prayer pulls us out of our lukewarm lagoons of complacency and plunges us into the incomparable life of God.

"Who are you, sweet Light, who inundates me and enlightens the night of my heart? You guide me just like a mother's hands but if you leave me I cannot advance a single step. You are space that surrounds my being and in which it is concealed. If you abandon me I fall into the abyss of nothingness, from where you called me into being. You are nearer to me than myself, more intimate than my inmost being. And yet no one touches you or understands you. You break the bonds of every name: Holy Spirit — eternal love!"

Edith Stein

The life of Jesus is the ground of our contemplative attentiveness. He impels us to goodwill. We make a liberated leap from short-time stays with superfluous or trendy groups or activities and settle into long-term, serious service within authentic social development organizations. Basing our ethical code on the beatitudes, we try to transform humanity beginning with ourselves. To examine the depths of what it means to authentically follow Jesus in prayer, we find out more about him, while giving him to others through loving service. The deeper our prayer life, the easier it will be to find Jesus in ourselves and in others.

Our work a day prayer supplies daily spiritual nutrients and sustains a contemplative awareness which wills us to pray if we are disinclined to pray. Reflective prayer is the vegetables and potatoes on our prayer menu. Contemplative prayer however, is neither describable nor a main course in our daily prayer. Even though rare, its effects can quietly sustain us for long periods of time. It might be comparable to an uncommon health-enhancing desert. After-effects of contemplative prayer hold a goodly amount of practical common sense. Mystery is present in all prayer, no matter what form it takes. Reducing the mystery of prayer to meet our non-spiritual needs is a serious miscalculation. As ministers of prayer, Carmelites set the fire of God's love upon the earth by fidelity to prayer. Prayer is a mystery of life that flows from God's life and gives birth to renewed life. Prayer is the foremost mystery and necessity of Christian life and always the soul of Carmelite life.

Mysterium Vitae

Mystery shrouds any mountain climb, as it shrouds our individual lives. What kind of person we are depends on how we respond to mystery. Mystery is everywhere: in injustice and fulfillment, suffering and joy, frustration and illumination. Where do these mysterious elements lead us? Our questing spirits must search for goodness and truth in everything that comes our way. Although this challenge seems overwhelming, with the help of grace we endure. Practical applications of gospel truths by the great saints demonstrate how we attend to negative mysteries in positive ways. By diverse routes the saints direct us to God, who is our ultimate reality and the greatest mystery of all. To probe the mysteries of God and of life is a fascinating and never-ending venture.

If we are properly disposed, God opens our hearts to the mysterious, lofty heights of prayer and compels our hands to humbly serve humanity. The mystical mountain top of Carmel reaches through cloud strata and is mysteriously hidden. Concealed, it beckons us, and we keep moving toward unknown terrain. One way Carmelites strive for the fullness of life is to reach out and grasp for things hidden from view. We give ourselves to Jesus and through him to others, often not knowing what our giving will entail. In prayer and unobtrusive service we reach out and grasp we know not what. We may be asked to do what seems to be impossible, but such are the ways of pioneers in prayer on a spiritual quest. Participation in the mystery of God takes courage and hard work. The integrity of the soul is as a new frontier. Courage is the ability to move ahead in spite of pain or fear. Although we cannot understand the many elements of mystery in our lives, their lived reality can be sources for down to earth, root cellar wisdom which spurs us ahead and also sources that keep us aware of the harmony of the moment.

The land of Carmel is lovely, lonely, exciting, frightening, intoxicating, demanding and even nondescript in its mystery. It is a land of agonies, ordinary things and ecstasies, which leaves dawdlers and whiners in the dust. The spirit of Carmel stimulates the deeper self to pursue the transcendent God with true ardor and live life beyond its routines and tasks. Carmel affirms life with the joys and sufferings that growth in love entails. Love, like mystery, is an enigma at the core of life. It has been said that the person who experiences the pain of love is the one who is truly alive.

We meet the pain of love in the land of Carmel, of this there is no doubt. It is present when we keep our commitments to love our dear ones, and pray and serve regardless of our likes and dislikes. As Carmelites we stand transparent, before a transparent God, for ourselves and others. We steadfastly participate in daily Eucharist, reflective prayer, the liturgy of the hours and devotion to Mary in seasons of feast or famine without regard to how we feel or what we think. We experience the presence of God transcendent in all dimensions of life alluring or unsavory as they may be. We listen to the word of God in the voice of the Church, comments from trusted people and in the cry of the marginalized. Since we are seasoned by our own deaths and resurrections, we continue to pray for those who are overcome by the forces of evil, never ceasing to remember that they too have souls.

The mysteries in life's travails have value beyond offering them for our own conversion, spiritual development or salvation. Although suffering can never be totally understood, it has always been an essential component for spiritual growth. A loving oblation to God of our own agonies unites them to those Jesus suffered in his passion. With Christ we continue the suffering through which he redeemed the world. If we truly live with Jesus in his passion, death and resurrection, we are a part of the paschal mystery. The mystery of the cross is the fullness of life. For many of us it is easier to identify with Jesus on the cross than with Christ in his resurrected glory. Accepting our pain with courage and confidence in God, and offering it to Jesus with generosity, benefits us and the people of God. We cannot comprehend the way in which this is accomplished, yet we witness it through the solidarity of people within the mystical body of Christ. God accepts suffering offered by grace-filled people for the salvation of humankind. Redemptive suffering transforms others by the bewildering mystery of love and transforms those who suffer as they grow in a special communion with God.

Indeed, pain is a mystery. However, in the spiritually mature person, chronic ill health does not express itself by drawing attention to oneself, or acting like an invalid or martyr. Instead, it becomes a channel for holiness as emphasis changes through an unshakable belief in the redemptive value of suffering. As we die to self-interest, we meet God in our pain and are free to be with him beyond the pain. A strong correlation exists between suffering well and growing in deep prayer. This may be because the progress of a chronic illness can prevent us from doing the things we enjoyed before its onset. If we take a close look, perhaps these things kept us absorbed in ourselves, or contained in our own wills. Chronic, degenerative illness has a way of releasing us from ourselves so we can abandon ourselves to God. Yes, illness magnifies our vulnerability and uncertainty about the future. A nagging sense of inadequacy replaces a self-reliant attitude. An "every question has an answer" optimism sinks in the stark reality of medical science because more is unknown than known about medicine. How easy it is to feel alien in a land that glories in physical fitness. Yet, despite the privations of chronic illness, we can continue to move around the many things which block our way. We use precautions and maintenance measures to preserve or increase our ability to function and guard our degree of health. If the negative aspects of pain harass us, we try to divert our thoughts to positive channels. This is no easy accomplishment. It is only natural for blue, gray or black days to come our way, but gradually divine love shows how harsh suffering purifies us, then becomes our mentor. A tiny light glimmers with wisdom: Each person is handicapped in his or her own way, and the worst of handicaps comes from a disabled soul. Indeed, even though confined to a home or hospital, a person can live redemptive suffering and embrace the cares of the world with strong and tender prayers. Faith and prayer do not take away hard times. They help us live through them.

When those we love are in dire situations, worry seems to be a significant part of our lives. However, as we progress to spiritual maturity, worry is replaced by concern. Worry and concern are distinctly different. Worry lends itself to judging how things should be, or how we wish them to be. Concern places those for whom we care in God's hands after we have done what we can. Vicissitudes are often what is needed for spiritual growth. If they force us to change directions toward a greater good, perplexing dilemmas turn out to be great blessings. They change the urge to rescue a person, to the desire to pray that the person may open up to God in his or her trials.

Learning to be comfortable with mystery is a slow process which is never completed. Therefore, we carefully avoid unnecessary solicitude about the affairs of others. We stop swimming against the dark river of our time as things usually unfold in their own way within the light of the ocean of God's infinity. We become more comfortable with mystery as we learn to float with the graces of wisdom in the waves of divine providence. How beautiful the passing scenery of life becomes when we really live in the providence of God. We come closer to Jesus as we approach him with childlike simplicity and trust, realizing that he desires the good of humanity more than we could ever imagine. Our plans and good works may be left behind as we await in trust for his plans to unfold. Yes, we must lose all that we have become in order to become all that we really are in the light of God. As Carmelites, we live in mastery. We gaze at the crowds and know humanity holds itself together through shared fatigue, suffering and, most of all, love. We are bound together in the mystery of human love and the Triune mystery of divine love. We receive the sacraments frequently, listen and meditate on God's word and are faithful to personal and liturgical prayer, but still long for that something more which we cannot explain. Untold graces unite our inner lives with our external activities and help us find and hold on to the will of God no matter what. Prayer is our fortress for renewal, a means for finding God and an utter enigma. We who live Carmel are like sleuths, looking for God in the most hidden of places, and living his presence by soothing disturbed feelings or unsettled thoughts of others at home or on the road. The unknown gifts we receive in abiding communion with God become, through us, part of the atmosphere in which we live. The Carmelites Edith Stein and Titus Brandsma brought the gifts of God's presence and love to their concentration camps, and Elizabeth Catez to her formal parties with young adults. Other people can receive these often unspeakable gifts of God without knowing their human intermediary or what the gifts actually are. Not so surprisingly, neither do we understand God's gifts to us. We abide in God toward whom we continually move. We have not reached him, but we live and move and have our being in him. We arrive at a place and realize we have already been there. How can we explain these things?

As we continually reform the reeds of our prayerful lives we link divine intervention to the people and places torn asunder in our world. Like the spokes on the wheel of the covered wagon we connect temporal journeys with eternal destinies. Divine guidance is necessary because human beings are unable to find answers to many questions on their roads of life. It is true that sound therapy and counseling are very beneficial. Yet, the deep roots of complex problems may be entwined in the regions of the soul, and accessible only to God's penetration and healing. No matter who we are, we need healing, prayer and God. In Carmel we experience a quiet wonder and joy as we pray for the world and those who inhabit it. We pray for God's glory, ask for his blessings, thank him for his gifts and graces and make reparation for our sins and those of others. Afterwards, our hearts rest in his love. The longer we live in Carmel the more we realize how we depend on the mercy of God. We openly and honestly stand before God, with the tattered trappings of our lives, and extend our time and weather worn hands to him. God places his merciful love in our empty hands. If we feel it is meager, we do not murmur. Quietly content, we share whatever we have with others. In the dry dust of our listless days, rock climbs of our routine days or sparkling delights of our glorious days we must always live by faith and rely on hope for our growth in Christ. Faith keeps our feet moving ahead and hope keeps our eyes fixed on Jesus. He is our steadfast rock who keeps us balanced in the ups and downs of life.

Yes, it is ever true: Continual travel on our mountain quest makes it more apparent that our hunger and thirst for God will never be fully satisfied here on earth. Rather than daunting us, this pushes us on, as we know our minds are not structured to capture or understand the totality of God. When words or images fail to identify him or satisfy us, ideas, theologies and dogmas become restrictive. Again and again, we must strive to release our own concepts of God in order to learn that we cannot see him and live. In his consuming fire, we interiorly burn away so that he can glow more fiercely within us. Truly, we are like ashes which are lifted, suspended, blown apart and eventually renewed in the furnace of his love.

9

The Alpine Peaks

Let us be one with Jesus. Let us make our life a continual sacrifice, a martyrdom of love to console Jesus. May all moments of our life be for him alone. We have only one task during the night of the present life — to love Jesus.

Thérèse of Lisieux

From time to time, we dwell in the stark caves of Mount Carmel. They are shelters of God's love. Within these quiet, dimly lit dwellings, we are more receptive to the gifts of contemplative prayer. The stillness helps us understand the beauty of receptivity to God who calls us to be who we are without veneer or defense. Alone with Jesus, in the quiet dark, we are more sensitive to what brightens or darkens our authenticity. Our pauses in the shelters of God's love allow us to be better signs of his love to the world.

Refuge is ours in the clefts of the rock. We cling to our rock of ages, the rock who saves us, as we hide ourselves in the heart of Jesus. As brief and poignant as these respites from the commotion and clamor of the world may be, they do increase our awareness of how much agitation from the secular world we absorb in our bodies, minds and souls.

By critically assessing our most alarming agitations, we come to respect anew the indispensable need of silence and solitude for spiritual survival. With Christ as our shelter, we can gladly let go of control and relax. Spiritual repose refreshes our weary souls where, in his abode, we truly grow by the benevolent nourishment of the silence and solitude. Quiet rest is vital, like a time of winter which silently nourishes the soil and readies it for spring. We season, as winter, in our cave so filled with Jesus' love, as we hear him whisper "Come to me all who are weary...."

In the gift of Christ's silence and solitude we are liberated from the limits of our finite existence to nestle in his merciful love. We have pulled down from the external battles of life, discords of the mind and disappointments of the heart. We lose ourselves in spiritual hibernation; it is a time of sacred latency or sleep. Passive and without fear, we let God remove the skins of our self-identity until we are metamorphosed by him. We no longer need our own ideas, opinions or descriptions about God or the sacred because the vastness of God passes through the fibers of our being and penetrates the very marrow of our souls. We are dormant and lie quietly in his all-wise strength. Sacred latency or hibernation is a serene spiritual respite that restores and refreshes a contemplative outlook. It clears our heads, while opening our eyes and hearts to the depths of our own nothingness and the all-embracing totality of God. When silence and solitude companion us to the deepest depths of our inner being, our false selves can be left behind, forgotten at the cave's entrance. At the center of the cave no distinction between subject and object is possible because we are immersed in the vastness of God. At this point, Jesus is truly alive in us since there is no trace of false self to inhibit even his smallest actions. John of the Cross takes us to the center of it all: "The Father spoke one Word, which was his Son, and the Word he speaks ever in eternal silence, and in silence must it be heard by the soul." Our true selves are in Christ where he gives himself to us in silence. How the mystery of silence amplifies the mystery of love. Jesus, hewn from the divine rock, is the rock of ages pierced for us. By reposing in the clefts of his heart we absorb how to reverence God and all life.

As the roots of our lives deepen in Christian principles, we blossom in higher Christian virtues. Goodness from our roots and scents from our blossoms waft through the fibers of all that surround us, even inanimate objects. Regrettably, so do the odors that emanate from those who are motivated by evil. We understand sightings from the beams of crossed wood that transparently reveal how love and goodness dilute the poisons of evil. We live Christian principles by personal holiness. Through our example we quietly infuse these principles into today's disgruntled populace. Hate is transformed primarily by sound Christian lives, and secondarily by instruction, assistance or guidance. Decisions motivated by hate, discontent or indifference can be moderated through the effects of goodness, wisdom, prudence and the waters of God's graces. How gratifying to know that minds can change and adversaries can become friends. When God's grace works through people it increases the quality of society as a whole. Marks of a sound society are located in its services for handicapped and elderly members (minority groups each person has the possibility of joining). Likewise, society makes certain the comforts and well-being of its people are not at the expense of the poor or oppressed. Holiness in the marketplace is not easy. Grace and determination continually burn in our lifelong quest for it. Indeed, holiness leaves the faint-hearted, starry-eyed or pious dreamer with their faces in the dust at the bottom of the mountain. The Dominican, Meister Eckhart, puts it this way: "Be in all things a God seeker. And at all times a God finder. Among all kinds of people and in all kinds of circumstances. And make it a life habit to copy Jesus Christ. To do what he did and to avoid what he avoided. Always learn to love him as he loved us."

A good rest with Jesus in the depths of the cave unfurls an ease in which we see the ideal of the contemplative lifestyle. Contemplative life opposes a disordered interior or exterior focus and anything else which impedes movement to God. A contemplative lifestyle is a hidden one, gallantly occupied with God. It is one of great love and great simplicity. Sadly, the well-balanced blessings and benefits from this way of life are almost unknown and rarely appreciated by people, even those in religious circles. Within the quiet confines of a contemplative community a preeminent love for God is manifested in a broader and deeper love for others. Whether living within a contemplative community or not, Carmelites actualize love for God through direct or indirect service. If the type of service is new or unknown, it presents a challenge. We try to bypass feelings of negativity or incompetence. We use our common sense and intellect and try our best. Even if we are good at what we do, we can become better. By allowing God to work through our vessels of clay, things can be accomplished which would otherwise be thought impossible.

Silence and solitude obliterate elements that hinder or entangle the soul's development. They increase the desire for quiet prayer which, in its turn, enlarges the area God has to work within us. When silence and solitude unveil hidden places within our souls, we can hear the quiet voice of God with greater clarity. Silence and prayer encourage us to periodically cleanse ourselves of old hurts and resentments. Being still allows God to speak in whatever way he chooses. Along with solitude, silence and prayer keep us in the absolute now, free of nagging past problems or future fears. The deep, quiet rivers of life are preferred to the noisy, shallow streams of existence. A centralized quiet decreases unnecessary peripheral hustle and opens creative channels. By putting aside all things we cannot carry into eternal life, we are able to act from the certitude of inner direction. Souls touched by God through silence and solitude are without parallel. Both life-sustaining forces reveal the journey of the soul as essentially one alone with God, supported by a strong, serene, unquenchable faith. By submitting to the transformation of grace, we truly believe God directs the course of our lives and illuminates our way, a few steps at a time.

Carmelites Refined

Rocky and rugged terrain bring to mind the breadth of vision necessary to authentically follow Jesus. The dense woods, rock formations, grassy meadows, hidden caves, mountain lakes, craggy cliffs and slippery slopes of our lives all have their own messages to impart. Each terrain offers space and a place to hear God's voice. Since we learn most about our uniqueness and value in the quiet of our souls, a soul at peace is reflected in sound motivation, speech and action. In the context of Carmel the gifts of silence and solitude are not occasions for selfish or self-indulgent behavior, nor occasions for ennui or lassitude. They are rare elements which can permeate the world and reduce its tensions. Blessed are these elements for their positive uses lie long in wait for more effective use. What we learn from and how we grow in times of silence and solitude, makes us better members of our families, churches and communities.

To be confident in God's love for us is to possess the courage to explore, discover and create. The knowledge and skills we gather enable us to love God more. At this point on the mountain, the spiritual journey is beyond pretense and illusions, because we do not need attention-getting behavior or self-flattering remarks to sustain us. Instead, we live our love for God by seeing value more than utility, and by calling others forward more than detaining them.

Even at this juncture on the spiritual trail, problems and setbacks prevail, but they do not disturb us at our depths. God is with us and we find peace at the center of our souls through him. We rise with him after our falls, go forward and find graces in difficult situations. We keep going after we reach the top of a mountain, because there are higher peaks to climb. The peace within our souls calms us when we realize that our times of great-est progress are those when we seem to make no progress at all. Indeed, we are not afraid as we look at our mountain map and find it does not match our surroundings.

Carmel offers a deep journey into God and we remain on this journey by vigilant prayer. To measure the depth of our prayer, we must measure the amount of love in our actions. Positive changes in how we think, and what we do and say, show us we are moving forward on the spiritual journey. Simplicity and honesty are the gentle virtues which grow along with prayer. Therefore we rarely expect signs, wonders or messages from God. Instead, we are gladdened by new spheres of Christ's love and new discoveries about his life. Lights from Christ brighten our way on the dusky, obscure path which takes us far, far away from the glittering, secular mainstream of life. Resembling marginal nomads passing through spiritually primitive territory, we face subtle corrupting instincts bravely. It takes great courage to keep battling with the forces of evil. Yet, we do so gallantly, so Christ's light can remain shining clearly in and through us.

One summer morning, a child stood in a great cathedral. As she gazed, the sunlight streamed through the figures in the beautiful stained glass windows, making these servants of God bright with brilliant color. A little later the child was asked: "What is a saint?" The child replied: "A saint is a person who lets the light shine through." The lights from God's graces keep us close to the true meaning and purpose of life, while revealing to us who we are and why we are here. Self-examination prompts us to change the things we can about ourselves and to give the rest in trust to God. It also prompts us to come to terms with our limitations and unrealized dreams. How often have we cast our expectant dreams ahead of the present only to arrive and find them different from what we projected? This happens in college, work, marriage and religious life, retirement and even in death. Authentic joy is found in the raw truths of reality, not the meanderings or infatuations of the imagination. Even though lights of future dreams accompany us on the way, we let them go when they do not become a reality. When we are patient with the ambiguities of life, they actually assist us to acknowledge, but not be controlled by, our fears. The hunger to be right, understood or recognized along with cravings, wants or ardent dreams can hold us back. When instead we burn with the fire that characterizes our passion for God, we can alter our mind-sets, attitudes and inner convictions. Quiet and graceful inner conversions provide the energy for reform in our external behavior and character. Life lived from the inside out circulates God's peace in us, and sends it out to the environment. His divine rhythm pulses within us and through our external activities. Blessed are we who enter and embrace the divine abyss of God which is within us all. Indeed, the fabric of our souls is fashioned by eternal, loving hands.

As Guiding Stars

One simple way to gauge the union of our wills with God's will is to look at how effectively we get along with others. Our ability to influence others in a Christ-like manner hinges on our sound practice of virtue within the fullness of gospel truth. Love is born of sacrifice, and sacrifice is a significant part of every life-giving decision we make. Our associates near and far are fellow participants in a reality for which we are responsible. Each of us will stand before God and will be held accountable for our choices in life. Therefore, we must aim as high as we can when we choose the degree and consistency to which we reflect the image and likeness of the Son of God in our private and public lives. We know well that if we remove the will of God from our commerce, business associations and transactions, all that is left is our will to power. It is quite evident that with no reality outside of themselves, people identify themselves solely by their own interests and desires for survival. When people adhere to work, or any other good thing, for its own sake it can smother them. Things become gods so easily. Therefore, the consequences of original sin are more evident in the marketplace where consumerism and competition undermine the values of human dignity.

In society or business, ways to make life-oriented decisions present endless challenges. A few suggestions are given with hope that the reader will develop others. A bit of silence before we speak gives the opportunity for reflection. This is particularly important before difficult evaluations or decisions. Because our differences make us unique, it is very important to show concern for all involved by an evenhanded treatment of all persons and their ideas. Sound criticism requires extreme love and gentleness as we keep in mind that love is always a choice. The mechanisms of self-deception are clever; knowledge can be used for folly and intelligence can be captured for evil. Conversely, sincerity cannot undo the reality of mistakes or poor judgments. Ever mindful of this, we should plan with prudence and judge with care. The active practice of common sense and religious principles in the public marketplace greatly decreases the weight of self-serving actions.

Honesty is best in any transaction, for business is a morally serious calling. Business people must take responsibility for the messages they put out, for when they do, they will have the public trust. Expedience should not replace religious principles. Right measurements of services or goods are a business person's pride and joy. Our careers on earth do not lie outside our Christian or Carmelite calling, but well within them. With God's help in personal or business situations, we know when to retain unity and when to stand apart, when to yield and when to resist. Surrender to God, through faith and love, must find expression in the concrete details of earthly occupations.

We try to envision the world through the ongoing, un-folding will of God. By nature, this is difficult because we are often more disposed to doing our own will. However, if we let our lower natures take hold, we regress from resolute prayer and advanced holiness. Although we usually have many reasons for doing what we do, good, sound and expedient reasons are often mixed together and are difficult to separate. We repeatedly see in our families, parishes or communities how easy it is for a person with self-willed pride to make petty preferences attractive or disguise good but selfish desires. Of course, we may not hear our own notable rumbles of self-aggrandizement. May God reward our soul friends who bring them to our attention. With a suit of armor and silver lance we take an alert stance and fight the subtle demons of self. Verily, we may think we hear the voice of God calling us to exalted deeds or blissful neutrality. However, if we listen more attentively it may be the voice of our own grandiose or lackadaisical inclinations.

The will of God works in us through grace and the responsible use of our intellect. The more we respond with appropriate love, the easier it is to live God's will. Our union with God hinges on our union with his will. Love keeps us in the habit of thinking before we act and responding in the best way we can to what we think God is asking of us. Praying or caring for others, when we do not feel like it, witnesses to a faith of substance. Such a faith keeps us faithful when we do not experience inner warmth and during times of inner darkness. Substantial faith is manifested in a dry yearning for God. We are sustained by faith alone, for our senses or minds may be muddled or numb. A dry yearning for God surpasses what we understand or imagine. A person living God's will resembles the catcher on a baseball team. The catcher is not inert as he or she crouches behind home plate. Seemingly motionless, the catcher waits for whatever comes from the pitcher. Awake and alert, we too wait for God and catch whatever he sends our way with open hands and a response born of common sense and grace.

Truths on the Mountainside

As Catholic Christians, discussions and disagreements will come our way. Such debates should be far removed from quibbles about petty differences or faults, nor should they be arenas for verbal attack. What it means to believe in God will be tested by our society. Divine truths are like armor in a gentle battle of wits. We do not create truths, we encounter them; for true knowledge of good or evil will remain true whether we believe it or not. Indeed, divine truths do not need our assent or confirmation; however, they stimulate us to pick God's values instead of the values of the world. Truth has an incredible attraction for individuals who are not afraid of it. We, who love, defend the beloved, but we meet our contemporaries where they are. Constructive arguments proceed without pounding our views and opinions into the ground. As concerns are carefully scrutinized and thoughtfully discussed, they can uncover points that strengthen faith. We miss the positive marks of debate if we raise an issue in order to wave our flags of verbal brilliance. Ah, how we can wrap ourselves in our own drama. Because history is strewn with discarded theories and assertions, we should not pose questions to preface our answers but probe deeper into the roots of conflict. At best, constructive arguments lead to the discovery of deeper truths together, while granting the opportunity to practice easy forgiveness. Truth exposes the steadfast link between forgiving each other and being forgiven by God. New disclosures define divine truths in a more refined context. A refined spiritual sensitivity places us in awe of God and connects us with each other without selfishness, control or manipulation.

When people rebel against the truths of God, the human condition worsens. God's love is the way to make sense out of the world. His love is manifested in sound humility, fair-mindedness and discretion. Love, as it flows from the channels of God's truths, is the soul of freedom. To confer with others about divine truths transforms us all. As we perceive a truth as best we can, we obtain a stronger grasp of the wisdom of God. Every perception of truth, no matter how small, draws us closer to understanding God, even though we shall never fully understand him. There will be times when our natural judgments take a different course. A hierarchy of truth shows that while any two propositions may be equally true it does not necessarily mean they are equally important in the scheme of life. A teaching about the nature and person of Jesus is of far more importance than a teaching on the nature and person of a specific saint. During moments of doubt or dispute, we trust the Church implicitly for she has kept the faith safe for centuries. The Church guides us into all truth through the power of the Holy Spirit.

The truths of God are the guides by which we interpret our experiences and the force that directs our behavior. Abiding in the awareness of his truths and living in his love are the foundations for fair, just and ethical systems in our society. A choice against God's truths is a choice for personal sin. Sin wears clever, eloquent and elegant disguises and is not dependent on our personal likes, dislikes or views. A sin is grave or less grave because it is so before God. Although personal sin begins with us, it always has social ramifications. No arrows cleave our souls save those of our own making. The wounds of our sinful deeds cut or split our souls and leave eternal consequences. Every sin is an injury done to our lives, the world's sanctity and God's majesty.

To know and love the truths of God deepens our passion for the truths of God to be evident in our society. We participate in this mission through a faith based on convictions rather than one based on emotions. By sharing God's love quietly, we become more alive to his wonder, beauty and glory in each person. We honor God by honoring each other. The beauty of love grows as it is given away. Although we are different in local cultures, we are all members of the same human family. The capacity for love, compassion and cooperation is held in common with all humanity.

Truths appear as we conform our minds to the realities of God. Truth, by its nature, unifies us with our authentic selves and with the souls of all people in society. Yes, truth brings together, connects and sustains life. Error presents itself if something we think as true separates, fragments and disperses.

As we ponder divine truths, we become more watchful of the ease by which we can bend the truth to suit our lifestyle. Conforming truths to our desires or actions is much less difficult than conforming our desires or actions to truths. At times, our desires and divine truths are at opposite poles and a lengthy grade exists between these poles. Desires which pull us away from divine truths vary in nature and content in each of us. We follow divine truths when our reason, conscience, faith and conduct agree and create inner peace. The truths of God are not decided by polls, votes, public or personal opinions, or views. They are beyond public or private sympathies or preferences. If we are unsure of what is true we can investigate by precise observation, assiduous data gathering and conscientious reading, consulting, studying, evaluating and praying. It is more difficult to see things as they really are than as we prefer them to be. From the human aspect, mutations of truth do occur. If one aspect is too absolute, we can lose sight of other aspects and a rigorous interpretation may result. If one aspect is too lenient, it can weaken other aspects and a lax interpretation may result. Assiduous study of divine truths maintains Christian perfection as a lively goal. Although we know we shall never reach it in this life, perfection is always in front of us as an encouraging goal for which to strive.

Our search for divine truths directs us to great faith in God. He may be preparing us for something we least expect. As we pursue truth we learn much about ourselves and more about God. Empty, stark silence often surrounds the splendor of various divine truths. Silence allows us the soulful reassessment of every aspect of our lives in the bright light and soul integrity of these truths. In the shimmering pure air of the mountain peaks, we see the real values and reasons behind what we do. We are directed to choose what we should decrease, discontinue, start anew or revive. When the truths of God refine and hone our lives, we learn to truly trust God's benevolence and creativity. To look upon the beauty of the Lord and the contemplative space within us as a sanctuary for ever-growing love, mystery and reverence, is to immerse ourselves in deep communion with God. Our contemplative space becomes more sacred as we recollect and cherish a specific truth or mystery of God. Perhaps this sacred space may even be the wellspring for some creative expression.

It seems that at the very depths of a Carmelite soul there dwells a poet. Poets weave a graceful rhythm around and through the mysteries of life. The imagery that underlies life crystallizes in the writer's thoughts and creates new life with words woven on paper. As melodic poetry rises from the heart, it magically captures the present moment and keeps it untarnished for future reflection. Poetry embraces human dignity and the common good and braids them with eternity. Through the ages poetic musings have assisted many along life's way. Simply put or profoundly expressed, words sketch how to pursue and wonder at the depths of that which is not known. A reflective gaze at the long view of life reduces living the status quo to rubble because many things of substance are lost in speed and efficiency. Poetic phrases reveal a sensitivity reflecting the nuances and vagaries of life. A long view adds the beauty of subtlety, serendipity, and fine distinction to a good journey toward a lasting end.

Spiritual poets seek the essence of life. They find flowers of hope in the brambles of humanity and those experiences stir the creative passions of the soul. Poetry celebrates a communion of who we are with what we believe. Carmelites are open to a wider view and heightened perception of life through symbols and metaphors that sketch spiritual experiences and truths of God through prayer. The most precious gift we can give another is a remembrance in prayer. Not unlike a poem, prayer is the gift of the soul. Poetry and prayer are sweet companions with silence and solitude as their guardians. The secrets in a poet's soul are myriad. A discovery of truth may gently urge those unaware of their poetic leanings to take pen in hand. One can sit at a desk, reach out to distant places and touch others with prayer, poetry and prose. Unlike an unexpected phone call, a reflective, well-penned letter gives the receiver time to muse, savor and read again. Yes, tender thoughts of the heart merged with delicate, gentle truths, are treasures to be cherished.

Truth is poetic. Everything fits into and reinforces everything else. A strong love for God in truth results in strong interpersonal relationships. The deep love we have for a few special people overflows into love for the strangers we meet. Simply put, divine love intensifies human love because God's love and truth are foundations for friendships of limitless depth.

Mountain Majesty

The intellectual and perceptual aspects of our minds develop to full potential when we pass through our reasoning and move into our contemplative dimension. The contemplative dimension is the spiritual center of an individual and contains reasons of which reasoning does not know. Herein lies our certitude in God's existence. Rarely instantaneous, our understanding of gospel truths and how they relate to current situations usually occurs after reflective prayer, profound respect for mystery, prudent consultation with the learned and careful exploration of possible options within a Christian context. Wise counsel clarifies facts, defines problems, helps develop workable solutions and expands our own expertise. Our contemplative dimension compels us to strive for sanctity by being more receptive to the beauty, goodness, knowledge and truths we find in God, ourselves and others. We become more forgiving of failures and weaknesses in ourselves and in others as well. With a daring orientation to God and belief in the sanctity of all life the sanctity of being amazes us with joy.

Joy is neither concrete nor something to which we can hold. It is better than that. Joy is something lightsome and brightsome which unfolds as God's will expands within us. Joy gives buoyancy to our burdens and amplifies our amusements. With ease, we appreciate what is given to us and surrender what is taken from us. Long ribbons of joy weave in and out of our lives in a sustaining fashion. Unaffected joy can surge through us unexpectedly. When Christ truly takes over our lives, the various experiences we receive through contemplative prayer are gifts of precious joy.

Authentic contemplative prayer is far removed from the popular usage of the term "contemplation." Rhetorical speculations or filmy interpretations are part of the popular meaning of this word. Often contemplation is defined, used, or publicized in inconsistent ways which tend to satisfy those whose interest is mild, passing or theoretical. Transient curiosity or fascination about contemplation is quite different from a lifetime practice of contemplation. Most true contemplatives are unknown to the world, rarely talk about their spiritual lives, and use the term "contemplation" sparingly and with quiet reverence.

Contemplation, especially within the context of prayer, is not something we do whenever we want; nor is it a way to see the world through rose-colored glasses. There are many kinds of contemplative prayer, each with its own gifts from God. These gifts are also unique to each individual. The kinds of contemplative prayer range from a momentary awareness of the beauty of the Lord to transforming union with the Triune God. Similar to life, contemplative prayer can be more than what we expected and better than what we planned. As we quietly rest in the mystery of God and passively wait for whatever he chooses to give us in contemplative prayer, we grow in appreciation for the gift of our lives. Contemplative prayer is given to us and surprises us with wondrous joy. We receive gifts from contemplative prayer, not as treasures placed in our hands but as divine elements through which our hearts are transformed. These gifts of unspeakable beauty flush into our personalities and become part of our being in ways mysterious to us. The surge of graces stills and mutes us. No one can adequately describe such beauty. Reception of these gifts shatters our defenses and enables us to surrender the deepest wounds of our soul to God.

The joyful gifts of contemplative prayer are mysterious and obscure. The contemplative dimension is preserved as long as we joyfully live in the presence of God and are consistent in following in the footsteps of Jesus. We discover anew the importance of this fundamental necessity, by moving forward on the Carmelite trail. The charisms of Carmel enrich and guide our contemplative dimension. The ego is blissfully left behind and no interference from it is a real blessing. Such a blessing leaves the human spirit free to expand according to God's designs. Truly, there is peace and joy beneath the multiplicity of problems and difficult circumstances of life. The refuge we find in our contemplative dimension keeps the pressing activities of our lives from dominating or ruling us. Neither compulsion nor addiction are reflected in our reasons for being busy. Nor is being busy a habit or an escape from serious thought.

A contemplative dimension enriches us as Carmelites by confirming our radical call to deep prayer. The deeper we move into God, the better we know what is of value and what is not. God's light enters the windows of our souls to the degree in which we keep our windows clean. With the constant help of grace, we can distinguish between what is a momentary fad and what is of good and lasting significance, and act accordingly. People who do not listen to God are prone to make currently popular choices. Because God is like a well-mannered gentleman, he does not shout in order to be heard above other voices. If people want to talk he does not interrupt. People close to the world rarely have ears to hear God or even others speak. Soapbox or windbag orators rarely bring us closer to God. In contrast, the amount of time or quantity of words is not important when we commune with someone who is close to God. Quality is the key because a quality prayer life is manifest in a quality presence. Brief encounters can be very impressive and momentary conversations most potent when we walk the road less traveled.

Contemplative prayer takes us deeper and deeper into the substratum of submission. Actually, we never stop learning about who we are before God, since he is more interior to us than we are to ourselves. Humility keeps us ever mindful of our own sinfulness. It stills the grumbles of the ego and purges impurities from the spirit. In humility, our graciously offered prayers to God are balanced with courteous actions toward others. We receive graces as gifts and respond by giving most of them away. Even things that disturb us bring us face to face with Jesus. Because we become ever more entranced by the person of Christ, Jesus uses our efforts in ways we do not know. His humanity is the source of our prayer life and understanding of divine life. The degree of our courage is dependent upon our nearness to Jesus. As we evolve into Christocentric people, our faith is more intense, our love more ardent and our hope more firm.

Unlike despair, which can easily shape our attitudes, hope is a quality of the soul. We live in hope with raw faith in the benevolence of God and the essential goodness of people. Hope holds fast when our feelings toward some people are much less than polite or positive. Life will ultimately yield its good to those who live it well.

Life's quiet blessings are as tiny treasures full of peace. The blessing of hope, like other blessings from a contemplative orientation, come upon us in delightful ways. The blessing of trust in God's goodness, works in and through us and liberates us from self-preoccupation. As we are released from rejection anxiety (a common form of self-preoccupation) we lessen the power of our adversaries or critics. Humility is the blessing that keeps us in spiritual shape. Weak spiritual muscles will hardly give our wings the power they need to fly to the celestial kingdom. Again we see how wise it is to reposition our hiking gear and change our pace from time to time, with the blessing of prudence. It permeates our evening's recreation as well as our day's work. A blessing of tolerance allows us to see each person who is marginalized positively and without pity, as we are all weak and wounded. A blessing of the funny bone is activated by the whimsical in thorny or difficult situations. Light laughter dissipates life's somber situations. Indeed, a good exercise for the soul would be a few laughs a day.

Dreary sights or boring places are in the mind of the beholder. Life teems in a drop of water or a motionless swamp. Contemplation reveals that boredom is a poor use of freedom of choice since any subject can be boring or interesting. Growth in a contemplative awareness of the presence of God heightens our sensitivity to the blessings of beauty around us when we linger and truly look at the tiny treasures in our day. A deep prayer life embellishes our appreciation of internal and external beauty.

As Carmelites we are not dependent on our immediate situation or surroundings for growth in prayer. We prove the validity of our prayer by how we live. Our routines in life can damage or deepen love's communion. If we live our lives in inner beauty, we beautify our external surroundings wherever we are. Carmelite living is not so much being in a particular place, as it is in expanding our awareness of how much God loves us. He loves us without reserve, each in a special, beautiful way.

Deep prayer and a high quality of life have an intrinsic connection. External activities are usually the result of internal aspirations. An aspiration originates from some point along a scale that extends from self-centered embellishment to pure divine influence. The more profound our prayer, the more our actions result from the prompting of God.

Ascent and Integration

Wellness in all areas of our lives, like contemplative prayer, has different levels of intensity. Wellness might range from very well to fair. The integration of wellness areas in a person's life might be superior, good, moderate or poor. Integration depends on a balance of external activities and internal decorum. Balance is not static. An integrated balance is a dynamic process. We watch our activities so we do not overload in one or two specific areas and end up in a crash. We watch our values, virtues and behavior so we meet a given situation with a Christ-centered response. We must be flexible. People cannot always be humorous or always be serious. An integrated balance calls forth the ability to adjust our temperament in order to maintain an appropriate decorum in whatever social milieu we find ourselves.

The contemplative dimension sustains the hope and faith on which we base our integrative balance. Hope and faith give us the resiliency to face a new day after a purgatorial event, and resemble a bright dawn shining with new life. The sunrise finds us back at work on what seemed impossible yesterday. A contemplative inner push does not let us give up or quit. True, we struggle in the nitty-gritty of our existence, but we do so with a buoyant wonder. A contemplative dimension diminishes troublesome influences because we embrace and live the teachings of Jesus with vigor. Jesus is hidden among so many things.

Jesus among us is powerful. He draws forth unexpected answers to questions which have long rolled around inside. Greater commitment to our daily concerns revitalizes our lives. Truly, we are unable to understand or be understood without God. He may escape the grasp of our thoughts but never the affections of our hearts.

The wild, untamed land of Carmel challenges us with an ever-adventuresome spiritual journey. We live it in our ordinary circumstances. Our lives remain witnesses to the truths of God as long as our ordinary ways are true to the gospels. The contemplative dimension keeps us unsettled enough about our lives to not become complacent until we reach the throne of God. Neither ups nor downs last forever. As we well know, a phone call or letter can change our situation in an instant. On the high peaks of Mount Carmel we can handle change with grace, conviction and integrity. When unforeseen events come our way, we may feel intimidated, but we focus our eyes on Jesus' loving gaze which pulls us to make choices that require the most courage. Simply put, we grow in holiness as we grow in love.

As Carmelites we are contemplative in proportion to the wonder with which we respond to reality. An ever-present sense of wonder is characteristic of the true Carmelite. The land we tread is ever enchanting! Somewhere on the mountainside we receive the gift of contemplative wonder, of holy pondering. We rarely dwell upon or talk about it. Nor do we use it for self-aggrandizement. Contemplative wonder is an outgrowth of contemplative prayer and essentially indescribable. At best we talk around it and are spare in the use of it. Who is adequately prepared to speak in detail of such a gift, so saturated with mystery and reverenced with awe?

Our contemplative dimension widens our prayer and deepens our yearning for the fullness of God. Union with God is never set apart from how we live the details of our lives. It bestows transcending value and eternal meaning to our tasks. As Carmelites desirous of a contemplative witness, we commit our lives to the Church by a rigorous internal conviction born of faith. Faithful Catholic living keeps us ever mindful of God's love which cauterizes our souls. His burning love helps us remain ever attentive to him, and the gauge of our attentiveness is how we tend to others. Tending kindly to others is of more merit in Carmel than speaking of our own faith experiences.

Straightforward View

If we stare into the face of stark reality, what do we see? Complete contentment is not found in finite things. A tinge of incompleteness, or perhaps even sadness, hangs in the air, even after an absolutely splendid day. A morsel of knowledge gleaned early on the spiritual trail was: A pleasure diminishes if received continuously over a long period of time. Indeed, the sweet is lost if chocolate connoisseurs eat a goodly portion of their treat every day. We often bump into our finite limits. Too often, life seems grand, then moments later, we turn around and stare up from the shambles of one calamity or another. Crime reminds us how quickly life is snuffed out. As Carmelites we appreciate the wonder of the here and now, but live by the infinite realities of God. Our works, good as they are, touch only a small faction of humanity. However, our prayer touches the multitude.

The search for fulfillment reaches beyond ourselves since the interior journey of Carmel involves observation, discovery, practical idealism, theory and spirit. It infuses new insights into the materialistic, temporal, pragmatic and utilitarian elements of our world. Pilgrims on Carmel's land meet God in prayer and active service, with preference for prayer. Carmelite prayer, hidden and wondrously all-embracing, aids us to be forgetful of self. Self-effacing prayer keeps our roots in God and sustains what we do with sound values and realistic goals. Prayer strengthens those who pray and those for whom prayers are offered.

The mountain of Carmel stands as a time-honored symbol of the spiritual quest. Even around the peaks, daily prayer continues, sometimes with spells of rigorous tenacity. How daily struggles test our mettle! However, we do not have the option to give up. At the breaking point, God breaks through and astonishes us. Holiness claims our lives as a gift to receive, love, share and give. While holiness consists of the wise use of our time and responsible performance of our distasteful duties, it also keeps our thoughts, words and actions consistent and in line with the gospels. Holiness points us always to the pursuit of God at the mountain summit. Of equal importance is the enjoyment of God's presence as he reveals himself along the way.

All Carmelites are fascinated by the Triune God. The higher we move up the mountain the more sensitive we are to God's presence. Exquisite flowers hidden among the rocks reveal his majesty just as well as picturesque vistas on the peaks. We carry pictures of our mountain inheritance inside us wherever we go. It inspires us to be signs of serene love and spiritual strength to the world. By also caring for the earth and all manner of things living, we are stewards of life for the One who created all that is good.

It becomes almost automatic to seek God's guidance in the days of our lives. Yet, rare should be our expectations of how he will guide us. Instead, we stand before him with open hands and hope in our hearts. At some point on our spiritual climb, we more or less come to terms with our imperfect world, Church, families, and self. Time after time we must work with grace through our disappointments and disenchantments. Somehow these graces transform us, and our external activities harmonize with our inner convictions. We do what we mean to do with renewed trust and robust conformity with the laws of God. There is appreciation for the wisdom of having no expectations. Love is the most excellent force that binds us to God. At the heights we love God gratis, the way he loves us. Self-emptying and sacrifices become a matter of fact.

We lean heavily on the wisdom and graces of Jesus, our traveling companion and goal. On the mountain peaks we walk in silence behind him. True love of another puts us in second place. Jesus knows that our self-emptying takes continuous effort and how we are still not divested of our self-will. As we grow in the love of God extraneous thoughts of self transform into genuine caring for others. We find we are kind to people we do not particularly like. We are helpful and stick with situations when we would rather bail out. Reality is much more than what we see or hear. Sensory perceptions of the moment may be ambiguous, over-stimulating, weak, flat or impaired. If we release what we momentarily perceive, we let Jesus draw us into stronger faith, deeper love and abiding hope. So often things so near us are not what they appear to be. As we look at ourselves from God's perspective, we see the person we were meant to be and strive to be that person. The key to wisdom is realizing how little wisdom we have.

Deep inside, we know divine truths are inseparable from the reality of our existence. The wisdom of God is inherent in all living things. As we transcend ourselves, we are transformed in Christ. His awesome mysteries touch all of life's moments. We find no lasting security in our knowledge, insights or work. After boundless leaps of faith, we experience security only in God. Our ascent of the mountain defies and surpasses any notions, however exalted, we had about God, yet strengthens our certitude in the reality of God and his truths.

Truths of God blaze in us after we pass beyond our own ways of thinking. The God of our imagination vanishes, as does the God of our desires and projections. The prayer of Carmel settles us into the crevices of Jesus' heart. Humility clears the way for Jesus to move freely in our hearts. We prostrate ourselves in prayer and let humility shape and remake us. Wrapped in silent mystery, our prayer leaves us interiorly mute. To rest in his presence and be absorbed in his mysteries is enough. Mystic showers of silent prayer saturate our hearts and minds.

Carmel weaves in us a pattern of deep fidelity and silent love through simple days of prayer and toil. Hidden sacrifices and obscure, selfless giving are as abiding praise to divine love. As Carmelites we must be living prayers. Since it is a marvelous privilege, we offer quiet prayers, day in and day out, for all who want to see God. The incarnate Christ is the center of Carmelite spirituality and we graciously let our hearts abide in him. Carmel becomes a way of life directly in tune with God's whispers in our hearts.

God invites all of us to enter into this kind of deep prayer. Prayer is a universal call. Without roots in serious prayer, no one comes close to a life based on gospel teachings and ideals. The New Testament and the documents of Vatican II invite us to seek and strive for the heights of holiness. Men and women of every vocation are called to deep prayer. Faith and trust inspire many to follow that call. A deep communion with God and greater holiness of life are the effects of prayer. The variations in the contemplative experience, including immersion in the indwelling Trinity which deepens into transforming union, are within the reach of everyone in God's grace. Failure to reach the summits of prayer is at the human level.

Carmel is a dynamic living of Catholic Christian life in a contemplative manner. The mountain of Carmel challenges us at our deepest depths and calls forth the heights of bravery. Our mountain, with its heritage of noble and enduring richness, provides a bold encounter full of promise. As Carmelites we scale the dauntless heights of sanctity and cast ourselves into the great abyss of God in ardent faith. We live in kinship with all creation and work so that everything moves in harmony with God's plan for the universe. Contemplation is not something in addition to being a Carmelite. Contemplation is a gift and a way of being a Carmelite.

The beauty of Carmel begins as a bud of springtime. At the price of long and costly effort, in time and grace it grows and blossoms as an exquisite flower. We lovingly respond to our call to Carmel by fidelity to love's constant giving. Jesus is our inner strength, the source of our hope and our fire within. Through the mystery of prayer and the movements of grace, we are filled with the utter fullness of the Triune God.

> Fall fruitfulness and golden splendor
> shine in light upon our pilgrimage
> through every year.

The settled fidelity of love's unceasing giving
is a gift known and possessed,
love does not consist, Teresa said,
in tasting sweetness, but in serving God.
It is an inner strength
that has passed through many winters,
and knows true humility, a serene trust.

Life in Carmel is a growth in love
drawn by the Beloved into that effulgent center
where he dwells as sovereign Lord.
His love's grace, like a fall glory
transforms us into himself,
and joy obliterates the deaths, the labors,
the monotonous hardships of the way.
And praise sings the glorious mercies
of the Lord of transcendent light
in victorious peace.

Take us, Lord, at the end of our pilgrimage,
as in the beginning,
and let our lives be a holocaust for the Order
and for the Church — tiny flames
to light the way to divine love
who is everlasting mercy.

Carmel of Terre Haute

Bibliography

Cummings, Charles. *Eco-Spirituality, Toward a Reverent Life*. Mahwah, NJ: Paulist Press, 1991.

_____. *Monastic Practices*. Kalamazoo, MI: Cistercian Publications, 1986.

Dubay, Thomas. *Contemplation*. Video Cassette Series. Birmingham, AL: Eternal Word Television Network, 1991.

Groeschel, Benedict, CFR. *Christ as Healer: God's Mercy in Our Lives*. Audio Tape Series. Boston, MA: Daughters of St. Paul, 1993.

Institutum Carmelitanum. *Proper of the Liturgy of the Hours of the Order of the Brothers of the Blessed Virgin Mary of Mount Carmel and of the Order of Discalced Carmelites*. Rome, 1993.

May, Gerald. *The Awakened Heart: Living Beyond Addiction*. San Francisco, CA: Harper, 1991.

O'Conner, James T. *Land of the Living*. New York, NY: Catholic Book Publishing Company, 1992.

Rosenfeld, Mark S. *Wellness and Lifestyle Renewal*. Rockville, MD: American Occupational Therapy Association, 1993.

St. Hugh's Charterhouse, Horsham. *The Wound of Love: A Carthusian Miscellany*. West Sussex, London: Darton, Longman and Todd, 1994.

Slattery, Peter. *The Springs of Carmel: An Introduction to Carmelite Spirituality*. Staten Island, NY: Alba House, 1991.

Taylor, John B. *Notes on an Unhurried Journey.* New York, NY: Four Walls Eight Windows, 1991.

United States Catholic Conference. Pastoral Statement: *An Invitation to Reflection and Action in Environment in Light of Catholic Social Teaching.* Washington, DC, 1991.

Walsh, Catherine Thomas. *My Beloved: The Story of a Carmelite Nun.* New York, NY: McGraw-Hill Book Company, 1954.

Walters, Anna Lee. *The Spirit of Native America.* San Francisco, CA: Chronicle Books, 1989.

Wilkinson, Loren and Mary Ruth. *Caring for Creation in Your Own Backyard.* Ann Arbor, MI: Servant Publications, 1992.